# Quick-Start

# Guide to Pocket

# Billiards

## STEVE MIZERAK &
## EWA MATAYA LAURANCE

### with Jerry Forsyth

D1566189

## Contemporary Books

Chicago   New York   San Francisco   Lisbon   London   Madrid   Mexico City
Milan   New Delhi   San Juan   Seoul   Singapore   Sydney   Toronto

1 2 3 4 5 6 7 8 9 0   AGM/AGM   2 1 0 9 8 7 6 5 4 3

ISBN 0-07-141520-3

Interior artwork by Jerry Forsyth
Interior photographs courtesy of the authors

McGraw-Hill books are available at special quantity discounts to use as premiums and sales promotions, or for use in corporate training programs. For more information, please write to the Director of Special Sales, Professional Publishing, McGraw-Hill, Two Penn Plaza, New York, NY 10121-2298. Or contact your local bookstore.

This book is printed on acid-free paper.

# Contents

# Preface

Steve Mizerak and Ewa Mataya Laurance are two of the finest pocket billiard players ever to grace the professional circuit. With more than 60 years of combined tournament experience to draw upon, these two champions have won every major title the sport has to offer.

Steve has been at the top of his game since the mid-1960s. In 1970 he won the first of his four consecutive U.S. Open Championships, and in 1980 he became the youngest person ever inducted into the Billiard Congress of America (BCA) Hall of Fame. His list of credits includes three World Championship titles as well as such interesting sidelights as TV appearances on "Wide World of Sports" and "CBS Sports Spectacular." He also appeared in two movies, *The Color of Money* and *The Baltimore Bullet*, and was introduced to the nonbilliard world in a Miller Lite commercial where he made an amazing multirail trick shot while explaining to the camera that he was "just showing off."

Fellow Hall-of-Fame member Buddy Hall names Steve as the best all-around player he has ever seen. Steve won the biggest events in 14:1 (also known as *straight pool*), the championship doctrine for pocket billiards during the 1950s and 1960s, and then twice won the biggest event in 9-Ball, the U.S. Open 9-Ball Championship. To date his name has been inscribed more than 80 times on first-place trophies in world-class events!

Ewa has been dismantling competitors since she was a teen-ager in her native Sweden. She first became an international champion at age 17 when she won the European Championship and has since won such titles as the World Pool-Billiard Association (WPA) World Championship, the U.S. Open 9-Ball Championships (twice), and the WPBA National Champion-ships. She is a two-time winner of the World Open 9-Ball Championship and has displayed her versatility by capturing the World 8-Ball title, the National 10-Ball Championships, the Nordic Masters, and the ESPN Team Challenge.

*Quick-Start Guide to Pocket Billiards* takes the combined knowledge of these two proven champions and presents it clearly and concisely. All players—no matter what their level—can improve their billiard game by concentrating on and mas-tering the basics that are covered in detail within these pages. Even on the professional level it is the adherence to the basic elements of the game that spells success.

Sharing the valuable tips they have learned in their years of competition, Steve and Ewa have created in this book a manual that will help even those who have never played the game get off to a quick start down the proper path. Here, through words, diagrams, and photographs, you will discover how easy it is to stand properly so that your cue can move naturally and effec-tively, how to aim to become a reliable shot-maker, and how to move the cue ball around the table like a pro.

*Quick-Start Guide to Pocket Billiards* will teach you how to understand bank and kick shots. It also will unravel the mys-teries of English and will explain the value of using defensive play, including safeties, to disarm opponents. You will learn how different table sizes will affect your game and how to sharpen your skills, even for coin-operated tables.

This guide will give you the tools needed to develop a firm and accurate bridge, a steady arm, and a deadly eye. Use the drills to build your confidence and develop your stroke. Developing the correct playing skills now will prevent the common errors that hold back so many players from ever reaching their proper playing plateau. All the teachers of the game agree it is easier to learn how to play pool correctly the first time than to try to unlearn a bad habit and relearn the correct way later.

This book is a quick, yet comprehensive guide, one that you can begin to implement in a single weekend, gaining the fundamentals that will stand by you for a lifetime of masterful and enjoyable playing. Use *Quick-Start Guide to Pocket Billiards* to polish your game one area at a time. It will take you through all the facets of the game in an organized manner, developing one skill after another. Each chapter builds upon the previous one, and combined they can provide you with all the skills needed to enjoy the game to its fullest.

# 1

# Choosing Your
# ● Weapons ●

*Breaking in a new cue takes a while. Even if it hits great, it takes some table time to build the confidence that it will give you what you ask for.*

—NICK VARNER

Pool cues come in an abundance of varieties. Some are such intricate works of art with complex inlays of rare materials and custom woods that they may only exist in a showcase. The menu of consumer-level cues is so large that to sample all of the styles available at any large exhibition would require many days. You will find there are as many different styles of cues as there are different styles of play of the game, and these creations range in price from several hundred dollars up to tens of thousands of dollars for cues that are more works of art than actual playing instruments. Since your tastes in cues will not develop until you gain a certain level of confidence at the table, the best advice is to become comfortable with the game before investing heavily in a custom cue.

Most of the poolrooms today carry a wide selection of cue weights for their customers, and most do a great job of keeping new tips and ferrules on them and keeping the shafts in good working order. Sample the variety there first where it costs you nothing. You can try a different weight or shaft diameter at will before investing in a cue of your own.

When it's time for you to pick your own magic wand, you will have developed a shopping list of the characteristics you want in your cue. Probably the most important of these choices will be the weight. The majority of cues sold today, more than 80 percent, are in the 19-ounce range although some players prefer a lighter or heavier cue. It is all a matter of personal choice that revolves around what feels best and allows you to be most comfortable at the table. (See Figure 1.1.)

Interestingly, years ago the most prominent cue weights were 20 to 21 ounces. But today billiard cloths are generally

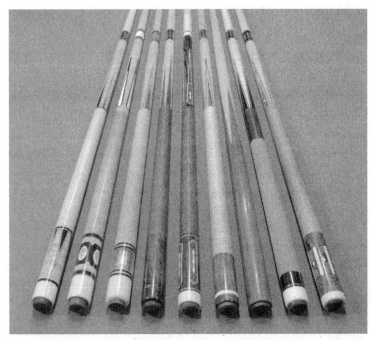

**Figure 1.1** There are plenty of cues to choose from.

smoother than they were then, so a lighter cue is required to move the balls around on the slicker cloths.

Also of note is that players once broke with a cue that was heavier than the one with which they played. They felt that the extra weight propelled the cue ball with greater velocity. That pendulum has now swung the other way, and today most players break either with a cue that is a little lighter or one that is the same weight as their playing cue so that it feels most natural. Whether you are a proponent of the "heavier cue hits with more mass" club or join the chorus of "lighter cues travel faster and propel the balls at a higher speed" is of little matter. Go with the break cue weight that takes the racks apart the best for you. Many players prefer a break cue that is rear-weighted since the cue stick is often held farther to the rear on break shots.

Break cues are a standard accessory for players who own expensive shooting cues. The less-expensive break cue absorbs all the punishment of the break shot. This punishment includes, especially at the higher levels of play, the extreme warping of the shaft at the end of the break, the flattening and "mushrooming" of the tip from the impact, and the wear on the ferrule and joint, also from impact. (See Figure 1.2.) Some players do, indeed, break with their playing cue, but never with ones that have ivory ferrules or joints. Ivory has a grain that may split from the force. Breaking with your playing cue will also mean changing the tip more often.

Another critical aspect when picking a cue is its balance, as diagrammed in Figure 1.3. Balance is determined by a variety of factors, including where you grip the cue, which is largely determined by your stature. There are cues that are rear-weighted, cues that feel as if they are front-weighted, and cues whose balance points appear to be in the middle. Each of these balance points has a large cadre of advocates who will sing the praises of their favorite. Listen to no one but yourself on this issue. A lot of balls are made with all of them. Try each cue and pick the one that feels most comfortable in your hand and gives you the kind of "feel" you want as you stroke. You may not be

**Figure 1.2** *Cues are tough!*

able to describe the feel of your "perfect" cue, but you will know it when it gets in your hand!

One of the most critical areas of any cue is the taper of the shaft. Most players now prefer what is called the "pro taper" where the shaft remains the same size from just behind the ferrule for a length of 12 inches to 14 inches. Others seem to like the billiard taper where the shaft taper begins right at the ferrule and expands slowly from there. It is all a matter of personal choice. A long taper makes for a more flexible shaft and a softer hit; a thicker shaft delivers what is known as a "hard" hit. Some players prefer "stiff"; others like the "soft" feel. Personal preference is why players need to try a variety of cues before buying one. There are many factors that determine the type of "hit" a cue has and almost as many opinions as to which type of "hit"

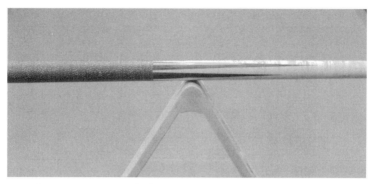

**Figure 1.3** *A cue's balance point is key.*

. is best. Steve Mizerak's playing cues, for instance, have by and large been "hard" hitters. They have steel joints and hard ferrules, and the hit is very "crisp" so that he can feel exactly what is going on when the cue tip strikes the ball.

On the other hand, Ewa Laurance represents a preponderance of players who prefer a softer hitting cue. They want one that translates the effects of the hit through a more gentle voice. These players are buying cues with composite (plastic) joints and with softer ferrules and even tips.

Another subject open to tremendous debate is tips. (See Figure 1.4.) There is a rainbow of choices available. And while most pros use a pretty hard tip, most pros also have no trouble contacting their aiming point on the cue ball and so do not suffer many mis-cues. Beginners might be better off using a medium hard or soft tip until they gain this accuracy. Local billiard retailers can explain the different brands and their playing characteristics.

As your game advances you will try different tips to determine which works best with your combination of cue and stroke. You will find soft pig-leather tips as well as tips made from water buffalo and laminates that are as hard as a shark's heart. Again there is no one right answer. Players from different parts of the world tend to play with different types of tips. One consideration is that soft tips flatten and "mushroom" from use more quickly than the hard variety. But if you are a

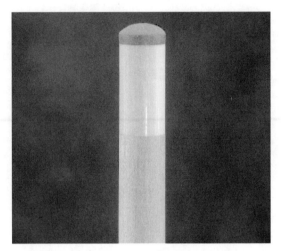

***Figure 1.4*** *A well-groomed tip.*

beginner and have not yet purchased your own custom cue this will be of less concern now than later when your game improves and you make that investment.

After you have decided on the weight, the balance, the taper, the type of hit, and the tip, there is only one major choice left, the grip. Most cues today are wrapped either in nylon or with Irish linen. Cloth wraps are designed to be comfortable and to absorb perspiration. Frankly, the linen does a much better job of this than the nylon, but it is more expensive. There are, however, other choices. Some players, such as Ewa, prefer leather. With leather or lizard wraps there is more friction between the fingers and the cue, so you can have a lighter hold on the cue and still maintain the same control.

Finally, consider pride of ownership when purchasing cues. Play with a cue that you enjoy holding in your hand. (See Figure 1.5.) Many players prefer a very simple unwrapped cue, while others prefer the multiple inlays and highly colored wraps that are also available. The playability of cues does not change with the amount of inlays or decorations, but the artwork can have a definite impact on how well you enjoy the cue. Decide what type of cue you want to own and how much of an invest-

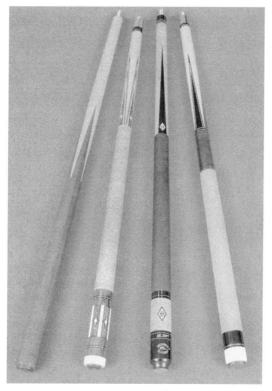

**Figure 1.5** *Lots of choices here.*

ment you are willing to make long before you walk up to the cue case. Just remember, beauty is in the eye of the cue holder.

Once you purchase your cue, remember that with proper care it will last a lifetime, but with careless treatment, it can rapidly warp and be ruined. Never leave your cue in your car. It can be warped by either cold or heat, and the moisture levels in cars change rapidly. Most cues are still made of wood, which absorbs moisture and expands and then releases moisture and contracts. It is this expansion and contraction that will raise the inlays on cues and warp the shafts. Cues are most "comfortable" in the same environments that you are. Try to keep them in the 68°–78°F range without rapid changes in temperature or humidity.

When you are not using your cue, clean it and store it properly. Wipe the oils off the butt and shaft and use a cleaner to keep the ferrule like new. Avoid "wetting" the shaft at the base of the ferrule with the cleaner as this is where the shaft is most vulnerable to damage. Remember that right under the ferrule is where the shaft is cut and the grain ends are exposed. Any moisture that slips beneath the ferrule at this point can be wicked into the wood grain and expand the shaft.

To store your cue properly, unscrew it and put it inside a lined case built specifically for cue sticks. Then place the case horizontally on the floor, as in Figure 1.6. The lining in the cue case will help control changes in humidity, and keeping the cues flat will remove most of the forces that lead to warping. Also note that if you plan to travel by airplane with your cue, you must check it as luggage. If it cannot fit inside your other luggage, get an extremely sturdy case that you can lock.

Whatever cue your hand holds is of no use until you learn to use it, so turn the page and we will get you started building a solid foundation!

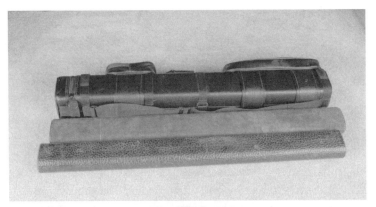

**Figure 1.6** Store cues flat inside a cue case.

# 2

# The Stance

*Put the feet in the right place and the head will follow. You see a lot of folks trying to line their chins up with the cue stick and stuff when the problem isn't their head, it's their feet.*

—BUDDY HALL

As in all sports, the game of pocket billiards begins with the stance. As shown in Figure 2.1, this foundation must be both comfortable and fundamentally sound in order to give the player the proper platform from which to shoot.

Let's go through this one step at a time. First, remember the goal—to be comfortable and positioned to properly stroke the shot. It is best illustrated by working in stages. In Figure 2.2, Steve is in the proper position to execute his shot. His eyes are over the cue stick, his body is not interfering with the stroke of the cue, and he is comfortable and balanced. He got that way in just three simple steps, which we'll explain.

Every new player needs to know about "alignment." Your body must line up with the shot in a manner that allows your

9

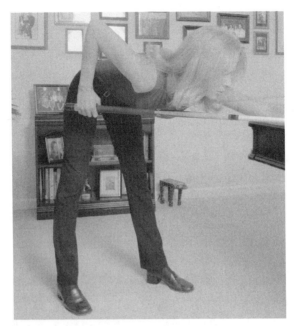

**Figure 2.1** *The stance is the foundation of the game.*

eye and arm to execute the shot. Beginners will sometimes stand too far from the line of the shot. Or, they'll crowd it too much and wind up attempting to lean into alignment when they stroke. This puts them off balance and really hurts their chances of making any shot. You need to be well balanced and positioned so that your mind can concern itself with the shot rather than being distracted by balance and gravity.

As with all basic elements of the game, utilizing the proper stance makes it easier to play and easier to properly develop the other aspects of shooting. A good stroke must have a solid stance beneath it in order to maintain the plane of the shot. It is simply much easier to play correctly than it is to play incorrectly. The following three steps will get you off on the right foot.

1. Line up the shot. Using your cue stick as a guide, stand behind the object ball and line the object ball

**Figure 2.2** *Comfortable and steady.*

up with the pocket. Then walk to the spot behind the cue ball where your rear foot will remain for the shot and use the cue stick again to line up with the contact point on the object ball. (See Figure 2.3.)

2. Now that you are standing in-line with the shot, take a step forward with the left foot (if you shoot right-handed) and point the rear foot outward about 45 degrees as Ewa demonstrates in Figure 2.4.

3. Next, let your knees relax a little and bend over the cue so that your eyes flow down the cue stick, over the cue ball, and onto the aiming point of the object ball, as Steve does in Figure 2.2.

You should now feel comfortable and stable and your body should be in line with the shot with no leaning or wavering. Your shooting arm should be able to swing freely without interference and without disturbing your balance.

This is the stance that has been most widely used in America. Other cue sports have their own stance formulas that are now being adapted to the game of pocket billiards. Snooker, in particular, has a different stance that still satisfies all the re-

*Figure 2.3* Line up the shot before addressing the shot.

*Figure 2.4* Ready to bend to the shot.

quirements of comfort and forming a solid base, and some mighty impressive names have had a lot of success adapting the stance to 9-Ball. (See Figure 2.5.) Snooker champions Allison Fisher, Karen Corr, and Steve Davis use this stance to play both disciplines.

The difference in the snooker stance is in the position of the feet. In the standard pool stance, the leg opposite the shooting arm is placed forward of the other foot; in the snooker stance, the feet are much more square. Many players believe this stance opens up their arm to the table better, improving their accuracy. Give it a shot, and, again, do what feels best for your own game.

Some of the pros, including six-time world champion Earl Strickland, mix the snooker and standard pool stances according to the situation. (See Figure 2.6.) Strickland believes that the two stances are in no way exclusionary to one another and that each should be used when it is most comfortable and can provide the best advantage. He uses the snooker stance for shots that require him to stand squarer to the table and the standard pool stance when he is at an angle.

**Figure 2.5** *The snooker stance is much more "square" to the table.*

**Figure 2.6** *Many time World Champion Earl Strickland.*

The goal is to adopt a shooting stance that allows you to be the most comfortable and secure while shooting. Some players, such as Hall-of-Fame player Jim Rempe, shoot with legs spread very wide. No instructor would suggest that anyone stand this way, but it worked well enough for Jim to get him to the top of the sport. Learn the basic solid stance, and in time you will adapt it to fit your own shooting style.

# 3

# ● The Grip ●

*You know you've got 'em when you see that shooting hand tighten up!*

—LUTHER LASSITER

The proper grip is vital to the performance of your game. Cue sticks are designed to transfer the "action" to the cue ball, to propel it around the table at your command. But if you grip the cue too tightly, the cue cannot deliver the proper hit, draw shots become impossible, and follow shots become unpredictable.

The correct delivery of the cue with a fluid stroke requires that the entire delivery chain of shoulder, elbow, arm, wrist, and hand be relaxed. If you tense the grip, the entire arm is tensed as well and the stroke can only degenerate into a shove that will never become consistent.

So lighten up! That's not an axe you're holding, it's a wand. Figure 3.1 shows the standard "three-finger" grip. This is a great grip for those just beginning to play the game. The weight of the cue is borne by the first three fingers of your shooting

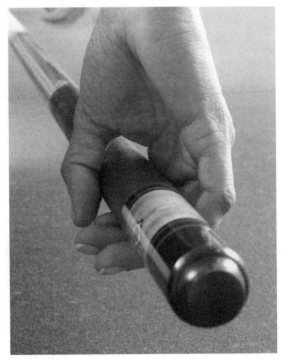

*Figure 3.1* The three-finger grip.

hand, and the cue is held in place by light pressure from the thumb.

Be careful not to exert too much pressure! On hard shots the cue stick should slip in your fingers on impact. If it doesn't move a little from the impact of a hard shot, then your grip is too tight and you are not letting the cue stick do the work. If you find yourself gripping the cue too tightly, as in Figure 3.2, you're making aiming and controlling the cue ball much more difficult than it need be. With the proper grip there is space between the heel of the hand and the cue. Also, do not get into the habit of gripping down on the cue at the end of the stroke to keep the cue from sliding. Let it slide. It won't go far as the impact with the cue ball will absorb the energy from the early part of the stroke and the distance that the stick travels after con-

**Figure 3.2** *Don't hold too tight!*

tact does not generate enough force to send the cue stick out of your fingers. Plus, there is plenty of friction between your fingers and the wrap of the cue even when it is just sitting on your fingers.

As you progress in the game, your grip will change to fit your own personal shooting style. Some players will opt for less pressure. Most will adopt the two- or three-finger style, while others will choose a little more contact and use four fingers.

There is more than just style involved here. The wrap you have chosen for your cue will also help determine your grip. A more tactile wrap, such as wood or leather, will more easily tolerate an extremely loose grip, while a slick wrap, such as pressed nylon, may require a firmer hand.

Your stroke will also refine your grip. If you develop a "punch" stroke, your grip may be firmer. By contrast, a smooth and flowing stroke allows a looser hand. Many old-time players, and even a few of the modern ones, prefer a "slip" stroke in which the cue stick literally slips through the hand as the tip travels through the plane of the cue ball.

As important as *how* you grip the cue stick is *where* you grip it. And *where* is determined in large part by your stature. A shorter person will need to grip the cue farther up from the butt than a taller player. This is because everyone, no matter what his or her height, should hold the cue almost parallel to the floor with a lower arm that is perpendicular to the floor. Figure 3.3 shows what your arm should look like when you are gripping the cue in the right spot. A taller person's arm will form the near-right angle at the elbow as shown, while a shorter person's upper arm will elevate from the shoulder to the elbow. In either case, the forearm should drop straight to the floor.

Because players are of different statures and, therefore, grip the cue stick at different points, cues of a certain balance may feel different to them than to others. For example, a cue that feels rear-weighted to a shorter player may feel center-weighted to a taller cueist who holds the cue farther back to achieve the proper arm drop. For this reason alone, someone else's perfect cue may feel clumsy to you.

Finally, the grip is the last relaxed extension of an entirely relaxed arm. The arm should flow easily through the stroke, with no room for tension anywhere in the shoulder, arm, elbow,

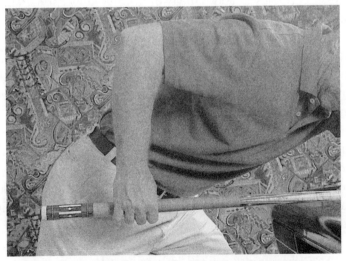

**Figure 3.3** *Position of grip is crucial with lower arm perpendicular to the floor and hand on the right spot on grip.*

wrist, or hand. When first beginning to shoot, don't concentrate on making balls, concentrate on enjoying what you're doing so that you can just relax. You may feel awkward at first, but just relaxing and having a good time will allow you to improve your game much more quickly. In all cue sports, tension is a dreaded enemy that blocks the progression of a player from one level to the next.

As you play, beware of common flaws. The hand should literally just "fall" into place beneath the wrist. Do not "hold" it in place or you may wind up "steering" the shot by turning the wrist under or out after contact. This will destroy your follow-through and make accurate shooting much more difficult. "Steering" often indicates a grip that tightens at the end of the stroke. The fingers tighten, and as they curl up around the cue, the wrist curls up as well. If you begin to steer, check your grip and hunt for tension anywhere in your arm.

As in most aspects of the game, it is not doing too little that harms the grip, it is doing too much. Relax and let the cue work for you. Think of the grip on the cue as reminiscent of holding the hand of a toddler—maintain control without squeezing.

# 4

# ⚫ The Bridge ⚫

*You don't really need the powder. You just need to go wash your hands.*

—Danny Diliberto

The bridge is the platform that allows the stroke to carry out the aim. So it is essential that the bridge be solid and accurate. There are two basic bridges—open and closed—with a number of variations of each of them. In addition, there is the mechanical bridge, used when the bridge hand cannot reach the shot.

Begin by becoming comfortable with the open bridge. This is formed by laying the bridge hand down on the table on top of a line that connects the cue butt to the aiming point on the cue ball—with the length of the cue falling on top of the same line. (See Figure 4.1.) Everything points to the contact point on the cue ball, so that the cue tip will be sent to that point.

The bridge hand begins as a relaxed fist. The fingers are then extended outward while the thumb is brought into the side of the palm of the hand. This junction of the thumb and the side

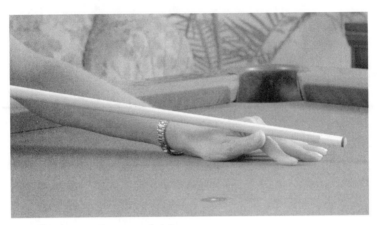

**Figure 4.1** *The open bridge.*

of the hand provides your bridge. Spread the fingers and thumb out as wide as is comfortable to form the broadest and most stable base for the bridge.

The open bridge should appeal to anyone learning the game. Since the cue tip and shaft are not restricted as they are when using the closed bridge, it is easier to spot stroke flaws while using the open bridge. The goal is to have the cue tip continue on after contact with the cue ball and end the stroke at a point extended along the line of aim. If the cue tip ends the stroke to the left or right of this line, then the stroke was not "true." Worst of all, if the cue tip winds up in the air with the cue being held there by the grip hand, then the grip was way too tight. At the completion of a successful stroke, the cue shaft will be resting atop the bridge hand and the tip will still be in line with the shot.

After becoming comfortable with the open bridge, move on to the closed bridge, shown in Figure 4.2. While the finger looping over the top of the shaft may make aiming somewhat more difficult, there are situations where the closed bridge is invaluable, such as when extreme stability is needed.

Form the closed bridge by beginning with the open bridge and then moving the first finger over the shaft to rest on top of the thumb. Relax while you do this as the other fingers will need

***Figure 4.2*** *The closed bridge.*

to move in a little, and the hand will tilt up at the thumb end and down slightly on the other side. Just remember to keep the fingers as wide as is comfortable to generate as stable a base as possible.

Both the open and closed bridge should be held at a distance of about 6 inches to 8 inches from the cue ball. This distance will vary from player to player depending on personal comfort. But remember that the closer your bridge is to the cue ball, the less room there is for a stroke error to occur. Do the math. The farther away from the bridge the cue tip travels, the more severe any tip movement becomes. So keep it close and accurate.

One of the most common uses of the closed bridge is in executing draw shots. On these shots, you are hitting the cue ball low and firm enough to maintain the backspin until after the cue ball contacts the object ball. The cue ball then stops at the contact and spins back toward the shooter.

The most common mistake beginners make with the closed bridge is not closing their loop finger as tightly as they need to. They leave too much "slop" in the bridge and do not achieve the stability that the bridge should offer. Take a look at Steve in tournament competition in the photos in Figure 4.3. You can *see* the tension in that loop finger and how tightly he is squeezing the shaft of his cue.

Since the oil in your fingers can make the shaft feel sticky as it slides through the tightly closed bridge, some players resort to playing with lightweight billiard gloves. Others simply wash their hands in hot water and use a drying soap like Ivory or Lava. Do not use a conditioning or moisturizing soap as they add oils instead of removing them. Get the oil out of your hands and keep them dry, and the shaft will slide easily through your fingers. To clean the oils from the shaft, use a damp rag and dry the shaft by rubbing it briskly with a towel.

*Figure 4.3a* Keep the bridge tight!

*Figure 4.3b*

*Figure 4.3c*

The open and closed bridges will form the basis of your game and will be the ones you use most often. But there are situations that require a little adjustment. One of these is when you must have your bridge hand on the rail of the table instead of out on the playing surface. The most common bridge variation used in this situation is shown in Figure 4.4, and it is one you should learn early in your billiards career. The cue stick obviously runs between the first two fingers, but you should always remember that the thumb is part of the aiming process here. The shaft runs down the side of the thumb that aims it and then through the two fingers that stabilize it. Aim with the thumb, not the fingers.

Sometimes the off-the-rail shots will allow the stability of a closed bridge. In Figure 4.5, Steve was in the unenviable position of shooting not only off the rail but also over a corner of the pocket. He was able to form a closed bridge, which gave him the stability required to execute the shot.

In fact, there are many variations to the rail bridge because there are many different styles of rails, which change from table to table. In addition, there are an almost infinite number of positions that the cue ball can land relative to the rail. As shown in the photos in Figure 4.6, you must simply be pre-

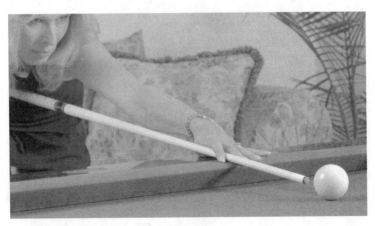

**Figure 4.4** *One style of rail bridge.*

**Figure 4.5** *Sometimes you should use the closed bridge style.*

pared to adapt to whatever situation is thrown your way. In time you will be so comfortable adapting to the various rail bridges that your fingers will assume the correct position without conscious effort.

Another situation that often arises is when you must bridge over an interfering ball. This is done using the open bridge and just raising the heel of the hand to whatever height is required, while maintaining the contact of the fingertips with the tabletop or rail. (See Figure 4.7.)

Besides the open and closed bridges, you must become comfortable with the mechanical bridge since there will be many times when you cannot reach the shot any other way. The basic rule of thumb in using the mechanical bridge is that the arm is

**Figure 4.6a** *Be ready to adapt your bridge to the situation.*

**Figure 4.6b**

**Figure 4.7** *Keep the elevated bridge stable!*

held parallel to the table. Take a look at the photo of Nikki Mataya in Figure 4.8. She has the butt of the cue resting on her thumb and her arm pivots through the shot from the elbow. The bridge hand is resting on top of the handle of the mechanical bridge to add stability, and nothing moves on the shot except the shooting arm from the forearm down.

Be prepared to vary from the norm if circumstances demand. While most of the time the arm is parallel to the playing surface when using the mechanical bridge, there are situations that may require you to be flexible. In the shot shown in Figure 4.9, Steve had to execute an extremely precise safety that needed a very light stroke. He felt more comfortable holding the cue as shown and did not allow convention to prevent him from doing what felt "right."

**Figure 4.8** *Nikki Mataya reaches a long shot using the mechanical bridge.*

*Figure 4.9* Break the rules when required.

Practice these bridges until they are so natural and easy that you no longer even think about them while playing. With just a little work your bridge, stance, grip, and stroke will all form a solid foundation of play that you can adjust as needs arise.

# 5

# ● The Stroke ●

*I'm constantly working on my stroke. It's the essence of the game, you know, and it's never static. You're always either getting better or you're getting worse.*

—ALLISON FISHER

The stroke is the absolute heart of the game and is where the game is most often won or lost. It seems so simple: just propel the cue stick through the plane of the cue ball in a constantly accelerating motion and watch the balls fall victim to gravity.

And yet no two players stroke the same way. Strokes are as individual as fingerprints, and more are flawed than are perfect. Players are constantly refining their stroke. Allison Fisher, shown in Figure 5.1, has won more tournaments than any other player of the last decade, and she is constantly practicing her stroke. She has worked hard to perfect her arm motion and is a great player to study for proper basics. Yet she is still working on it.

*Figure 5.1* Consistent tournament winner Allison Fisher
lines up a shot.

It is the stroke that you see begin to break down even in champions during big matches. When the nerves kick in, the normally relaxed arm can become clumsy from tension. And once that fundamental requirement of relaxation is gone, the stroke begins to fall apart. The stroke in pool is just as important as it is in golf. In both games you must deliver your stick properly and go through the plane of the ball aligned with the shot, ending with a smooth follow-through.

The perfect stroke feels something like this: imagine you have a beanbag tucked in your shooting hand and resting on your fingers as a cue would be. (See Figure 5.2.) If you just toss that bag underhanded across a 10-foot room, you have felt what the proper stroke should feel like.

The bag was loose in your hand, and your arm accelerated all the way to the end. Your arm and all of its components were relaxed. Now stand in a billiard stance, bend over as if to shoot, and imagine tossing that beanbag again. Begin with the hand hanging loose and falling in a straight drop toward the floor.

Bring the swing back about 6 inches to 8 inches, pause at the end of the backswing to allow the biceps to take over from the triceps, and then "toss the bag," accelerating until your hand is stopped by running into your chest. If you can do that with a cue in your hand, you may be the next world-beater!

Let's go through this one step at a time. But consider all these steps only when practicing. When you are playing you should assume that you are doing just what you do in practice and trust your arm to do the right thing. If it does not, go back to the practice room where you can work on the various segments of the stroke. Concentrating on them while playing will only steal your attention from aiming.

Prior to the actual shot stroke you will take a series of warm-up strokes. It is important to understand the purpose of these warm-ups. By the time you actually begin these strokes you will have already decided exactly what you must do on the shot. You know precisely where the object ball is going, and you know where the cue ball is going. All that is left is to carry out the plan.

**Figure 5.2** *Toss a beanbag underhanded to get the feel of a perfect shot.*

The warm-ups are your opportunity to practice the speed of the shot that you are undertaking, to get the arm moving back and forth exactly as you imagine that it will on the shot itself. But they are much more than that. They are also your chance to relax as much as possible and to focus. Once you have bent to the shot, your world should only exist within the rails. While the arm swings back and forth, reassure yourself of the certainty of making this shot and getting shape on the next one. Reinforce your resolve to be successful. Once you have focused entirely on the task at hand and have relaxed, you are ready to begin the actual shot stroke.

The first position of the stroke is called the "set" position. This is the cue position that you relax into after you have taken your warm-up strokes and immediately prior to taking the shot stroke. Ideally, the top of the shooting arm and the cue stick are parallel to the floor while the forearm is perpendicular to them. This 90-degree angle of the elbow allows the stroke to flow from the elbow with only the lower arm executing the shot. However, as seen in Figure 5.3, players of shorter stature may be required to raise the upper arm beyond parallel alignment

**Figure 5.3** *The set position.*

in order to maintain the all-important perpindicular drop of the lower arm.

The most common description is that the lower arm acts similar to a pendulum. On most shots there should be no movement of the body or the arm above the elbow. Movement in the body is a basic flaw and is yet another example of "doing too much." Again, relax and enjoy feeling the lower arm do all the work. The lower arm is also relaxed, but controlled to move in a straight line and to accelerate through the follow-through of the shot.

The second position is the "pause" position. (See Figure 5.4.) This is the point in the stroke when the hand is farthest to the rear. As in golf, do the backswing slowly, being careful to keep the cue in line with the shot. At the end of the backswing there is a tiny pause, almost imperceptible in most players, that allows the stroke to transfer from going backward to going forward. This is where the biceps take over control of the cue from the triceps, which executed the backstroke.

Now is where the discipline of relaxing really kicks in. Do not move the body toward the shot! Just stay still and let the arm

**Figure 5.4** *The pause position.*

deliver the cue. (See Figure 5.5.) It is best to practice this at first with no cue ball on the table, just stroke through the air. Imagine you are tossing that beanbag, and just let the arm carry the cue through until your thumb stops at your chest and the cue tip is touching the felt. Because the arm travels in an arc, the cue tip will fall to the felt as your arm finishes the stroke. No matter. If your "set" position was true, the cue stick was on a level plane when it went through the cue ball.

Stay down! Unless you must move to avoid being hit by a traveling ball, practice "freezing" in the finish position until the object ball drops into the pocket and the cue ball stops moving. Staying down is a vital part of the follow-through section of the stroke. You will often hear pros telling one another "you jumped up on it" when they have missed a shot.

That's it! Set, pause, and finish. In practice, concentrate on those three components. But in game play concentrate only on the aim and on relaxing. Develop early on the habit of trusting your arm to deliver what you need. Don't ever try to force the arm. That generates tension, and tension is the giant-killer of pool. In this game you generate power by moving the cue stick quicker, not by pushing it harder.

**Figure 5.5** The finish position.

# 6

# Aiming

*When you're hot everything just goes on autopilot, so all you have to focus on is the aiming.*

—Francisco Bustamante

Aiming is the one area of pocket billiards you will concentrate on most diligently while playing the game. Possessing an excellent set of basic mechanics is requisite to delivering the cue ball properly, but it is useless unless the aim is solid. Luckily, aiming is one of the easiest obstacles a pool player must cross. And, in time, it will become so automatic that you stop being overly concerned about it—you just perform. It is much like a beginning violinist who struggles with each finger placement at first but who soon finds the fingers fall naturally onto the proper fretting.

There are two basic ideas you need to grasp. One is *contact point* and the other is the *ghost ball*. All you need to know about the contact point is how small it is; therefore, your aim must be precise enough to focus on that point. To understand this, just

**Figure 6.1** *The aiming, or contact, point is tiny!*

take two billiard balls and hold them up in front of a bright window and look at their contact point. You will find that it is tiny. (See Figure 6.1.) Keep this information in the back of your mind for now. What you must remember is that it does no good to aim at a point on the object ball that is the size of a nickel when the contact point is really the size of a pinhead. You can hit inside the "nickel" point and still miss shots all day long.

It's time to learn the granddaddy of all aiming systems— the *ghost ball*. This system has the pupil imagining a cue ball sitting next to the object ball in perfect alignment to pocket the shot. The task of aiming, then, is to replace the imaginary cue ball with the real thing by shooting the real cue ball into the space occupied by the ghost ball. Succeed at that and you make every shot, every time!

The basic premise of this aiming system is that the ghost cue ball is lined up so that a line drawn through the center of both it and the object ball runs right into the center of the pocket, as shown in the diagram in Figure 6.2. No matter where the object ball and pocket are in relation to one another, if you can drive the cue ball into position where a line drawn through its center and then through the center of the object ball lines up with the pocket, then the shot can be made.

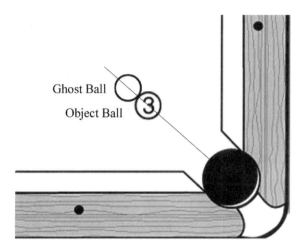

*Figure 6.2* The ghost ball.

The ghost ball system can really help with "thin" cuts. While straight-in shots are easy to understand, many beginning players have some trouble with "thin" cuts. They quickly see how nearly straight-in shots are made but become confused when they try to cut balls very thin. Here's where you can use the ghost ball system to your advantage.

The shot diagrammed in Figure 6.3 can be made into the corner pocket. This is nearly a straight-in shot and obvious to

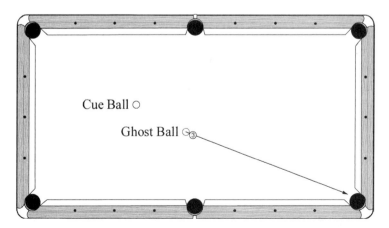

*Figure 6.3* A straight-in cinch.

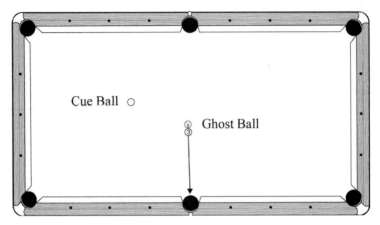

**Figure 6.4** A thin cut.

everyone. But the shot can also be made in the side pocket, as
shown in the diagram in Figure 6.4. This is a much thinner cut,
but it can still be made fairly easily once you see the position
of the ghost ball and just replace the ghost ball with the real
thing.

The path to the most obvious pocket will often be blocked
or it will be a path that allows you no way to get into good position for the next shot. Being able to unleash that thin cut shot
can get you through a lot of hard times. So how thin is too thin?
Ninety-one degrees is too thin. Take a look at the diagram in
Figure 6.5. As you can see, in this exaggerated example, a ghost
ball placed beyond the 90-degree angle point is useless because
you can no longer drive the real cue ball into that position. The
edge of the object ball simply prevents you from getting there.
And that edge is the limit. You can hit the object ball on its very
outer edge (the 90-degree point) and make shots all day long.
But you cannot go even one degree farther, or the edge of the
object ball will block you. Remember: If the shot angle is 90
degrees or less you can make the shot. More than that and you
are looking at either a safety or a kick or a bank.

This means you actually have 180 degrees, or half, of the
object ball to consider—90 degrees on each side of straight on.
(All right, we know that somewhere there is a physicist who is

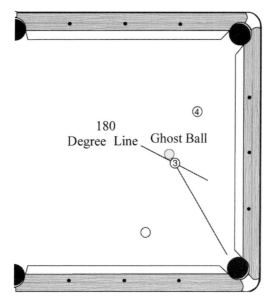

**Figure 6.5** *You can't get there from here.*

going to take us to task because the actual available portion of any object ball is slightly less than 180 degrees since the end limits of that angle are reduced by the respective widths of the cue ball and the object ball. Yes, that's correct. Let us continue.) The half of the ball that is facing you is all fair game for cue ball contact and making shots, as shown in the diagram in Figure 6.6. Conversely, any aiming point on the dark side of the moon (the 180 degrees that is not facing you) is out of the equation.

As you can see from these diagrams, it is extremely rare for the cue ball and the object ball to be lined up dead straight-on into the pocket. Most of the time your shots will involve some degree of angle. This just means that it is rare that you are aiming the center of the cue ball to strike the object ball. In fact, you almost never are. When you aim a straight-in shot, you are just using the centerline of the cue ball to line up the edge of the cue ball with the contact point on the object ball. It is mostly the edges of the balls that make contact with one another, rarely the centers.

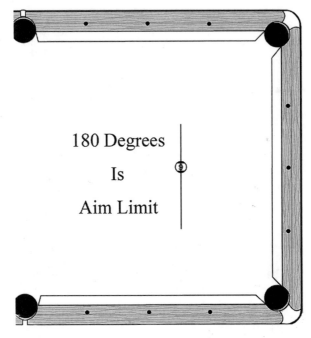

**Figure 6.6** No more than 180 degrees.

Your next step is to get on the table and start replacing the ghost ball with the cue ball. If you are a center-ball freak, fine, just shoot to replace the center of the ghost ball with the center of the cue ball and the edges will take care of themselves! In short, don't overcomplicate this step. The physics of colliding spheres is not rocket science. Just relax and have a good time adjusting your aim, and you will progress at a rapid rate. The art of aiming is developing a good "feel" for when you are in-line, not from understanding the various intricate geometries of the game. And you will develop this feel with table time. The best players in the world never think about how many degrees of an arc their aim encompasses. They just know (from countless hours of play) when they are lined up and when it is time to pull the trigger.

The photos in Figures 6.7 and 6.8 show a method that Ewa has used very successfully with her students to demonstrate the effectiveness of the ghost ball. When showing her daughter,

***Figure 6.7*** *First, aim at the ghost ball.*

***Figure 6.8*** *Then lift away the ghost ball and complete the shot.*

Nikki, how to aim, Ewa first has Nikki line up her cue ball to send it to the point on the table where the ghost ball (the 3-ball) rests. Then, after Nikki is sure of her aim, Ewa simply removes the ghost ball from the table and allows Nikki to shoot. If her aim was true, the shot will fall every time.

The hurdle to overcome early on is frustration. You are not going to start out by pocketing all the balls that you line up upon. You are going to miss. The key is to laugh at these early misses and just keep playing and enjoying yourself. If you understand the premise of the ghost ball aiming system and just keep that in the back of your mind as you play, the balls will begin going in more and more often. You even will refine your aim as a matter of course. Don't worry about it. Enjoy yourself at the table, and the balls will begin to disappear into the pockets.

There is one key you should always remember about aiming, and it is simple. Most balls that are missed by the accomplished players of the game are not a result of bad aiming, but a consequence of an improper stroke, stance, or grip. It matters very little if you are aiming properly, if the cue stick is wandering through the plane of the cue ball similar to an unruly drunk. The importance of developing your solid basics of stance, grip, and stroke, covered in earlier chapters, simply cannot be overstated. They will step up to slap you much more often than will your aim.

When pros go into a slump it is not their aim that they question. First they check their stance (and how they get there, the address), and then they work on their stroke. What they want to know about their grip is whether or not they are unconsciously tightening down. Sometimes nerves will do this to you in a big game, and it can be the kiss of death since a tight wrist cannot deliver a smooth and true stroke.

One of the Billiard Congress of America (BCA) Master Instructors, Randy Goettlicher of Dallas, has said, "When advanced players come to us for help they almost always tell us that they have an aiming problem. They rarely do. Aiming is really too simple for them to have a problem with. Their problems almost always revolve instead around one of the three basics of stance, grip, or stroke. Once we show them how to get back to the proper basic, the 'aiming problem' resolves itself. The aim cannot be true and consistent if the basics are not followed."

Ewa checks her stroke versus aim equation by stroking her cue down the rail of the table, just above the line created where the cloth tucks under the rail. (See Figure 6.9.) The straight line provided by the table allows her to easily see if her stroke is as straight as she needs. If the cue tip remains above the line as she strokes, then she knows whatever problem has arisen is *not* the result of an errant stroke.

So, is that all there is to aiming? Just imagining that the ghost ball is lined up with the pocket and replacing it with the cue ball? Yes, that's it. Entire tomes of great verbage have been penned to describe aiming in billiards, but it all just boils down

**Figure 6.9** *Stroke atop a straight line to check yourself.*

to striking the object ball at the point opposite the pocket to send it tumbling into the hole.

At some point in your game you will begin to get concerned with deflection (the deviation from the desired straight line of the cue ball caused by hitting it off-center with English). But you will find most of these concerns contain more smoke than flame. Sure, the cue ball will squirt to the right when you hit it on the left and vice versa. But your marvelous brain will see this effect whether or not you have an in-depth understanding of it, and it will make the required adjustments in your aim without you even being aware of the process.

Don't worry about all of the complexities that you will hear people discussing about aim. Put the cue ball where the ghost ball sits and you will be making shots while they are arguing over stiff shafts, whippy shafts, and the nap of the cloth. Life is tough enough without trying to understand the complexities of respiration. Just breathe, enjoy the fragrance of the flowers, and get on with your day.

However, before we send you merrily out onto the slate, there is one aspect of the game that you should begin considering now. *Visualization.* From this point on we are going to be talking a lot about visualizing the shot prior to execution, and aim is part of that visualization. Before you ever bend to the table, you should "see" the shot take place successfully in your mind. Just imagine the cue ball leaving your cue tip and traveling perfectly on-line, striking the object ball precisely, and then parting company with the object ball as that ball goes into the pocket while the cue ball travels to the point on the table you need to execute the next shot. Visualize. See everything happen before you pull the trigger, and, with the proper technique, your ball will find its target.

# 7

# Basic
● Position Play ●

*Anybody can make a shot. The trick is to make the next one.*
—BUDDY HALL

Making one shot in the game of pool is of no real value. Winning at any game requires making multiple balls, and the idea is to make them in as few trips to the table (innings) as possible. This means on every shot you must not only make the ball at which you're aiming, but you must also roll the cue ball into a spot where you can make another shot, and another, and another. When players speak of being "in control," they're referring to their position play.

The ability to achieve position is what truly sets champion players apart. They can all make the tough shots. You will get to a point in your play where shot-making becomes the least of your concerns. It is steering that white ball around the table that separates the winners from all the others. When you watch champions playing, you often hear people comment on how simple it looks. That is how it should be. You should have at most one tough shot per game, usually the first one. Use that shot to get into line, and if you stay there the game is yours, just one simple shot after another.

While sometimes the table layout is so difficult that several hard shots are required to get through the rack, in general when you see players executing one tough shot after another, you are seeing players work harder than they should. These are players who have been unable to get into line. The best players do not pull off miracle shot after miracle shot because they play position so well that the majority of their shots are easy. And this is where visualization comes into play—you have to visualize your position play *before* you step to the table to shoot. While you are still standing back from the table and looking at the shot, imagine the path the cue ball must take to get to the next shot and "see" it follow that track in your mind.

Suppose you have the shot diagrammed in Figure 7.1. The 3-ball has to go into the corner pocket and the cue ball has to go two or three rails to get shape on the 4-ball and land within the target area. For simplicity, the rest of the balls have been removed from the table. Later in this chapter, we'll give you the tools to get the cue ball to obey your imagination, but for right now just imagine the path that the cue ball must take, as diagrammed.

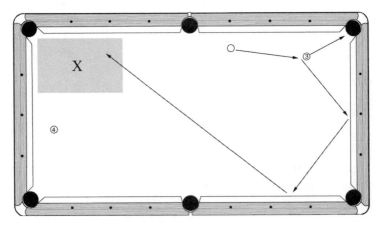

**Figure 7.1** *The multirail position shot.*

Next you must communicate this path to your arm. This is where many players make their first deadly error. They try to "engineer" the ball around the table. In their mind, they're saying, "OK, first I strike the object ball at the contact point, then travel 18 inches to the foot rail, come off to the side rail 23 inches away, and then travel 80 inches across the table at an angle of 45 degrees to the third rail. I must rebound 3 more inches off of that rail and then stop. So, figuring that the stint factor of this cloth is X then the cue ball must be propelled at Y mph with no English."

Then they try to "tell" their arm to do all that. Impossible. Even a genius such as Albert Einstein couldn't pull that shot off, and neither can any pro pool player in the world. But, there is no need to do any of that figuring because you have a brain that responds to pictures. Just compare playing pool with driving a car. To turn a corner while driving, all you have to do is see the angle of the corner. Your arm turns the wheel just the right amount to make the corner as you desire. You do not calculate how many degrees to turn the wheel to make this particular corner, you just see it and go. You "react" visually to the corner and respond with the muscle movements to navigate it properly. We're talking about the same process in pool when we say "imagine the shot." If we weren't able to learn from visualization, the game would be too complex to master. But, fortunately, all we have to do to make a shot is to picture it properly and trust our arm, just as we do when driving a car.

And here is another vital key: visualizing is easier to do if you are relaxed and happy than if you are uptight and strict. So enjoy the game. Having fun while you play is basic to learning quickly. When you stop grinning at the table, you have reached the point of diminishing returns. Go put the stick up and come back another day.

Once you start visualizing accurately and you begin to "see" the shots and expect the ball to go where you imagine, the true learning process begins. (See Figure 7.2.) You will start to make subconscious adjustments on every shot that will improve your

**Figure 7.2** *Many players draw mental white lines to see the paths.*

odds of making that shot again. If you imagine the cue ball leaving the object ball at one angle and it leaves at another, your subconscious will store that information away and make an adjustment the next time you shoot a similar shot. No need to "work" this process; just let it happen. Visualize the shot beforehand, and your brain will compare that picture to what actually happens when you shoot.

If the cue ball comes off the rail too short, then the next time your mind will guide that cue tip just a little farther out toward the edge of the cue ball to get a little more spin. If you come up short of pace, then next time the arm will move a little faster. Come up long, and it will slow next time. You will learn to relax and trust your arm. Given enough repetitions, that arm will become uncannily accurate as its friend—the subconscious—

becomes more and more skilled and relaxed at guiding its motion.

This is the fastest way to learn and to progress at position play. Leave all your engineering skills at the office, and use your visualization skills and imagination to craft your position play in pool. (See Figure 7.3.) This game is easily as much art as science. There are, of course, ways to learn that are much faster than others, so let's get into those now.

First, repetition is key. Set up that 3-ball shot and shoot it time and time again until you not only make the 3-ball but also have a great shot on the 4-ball. Each time you go to the wrong spot on the table, ask yourself what the cue ball needs in order

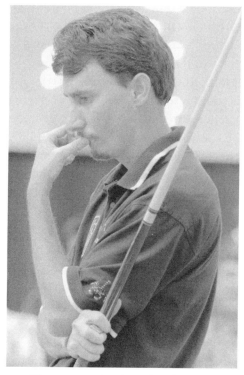

***Figure 7.3*** *Visualize the shot first, as Johnny Archer does.*

to make it go along the proper path. Then make the adjustment and shoot again. Practicing the same shot over and over allows your muscle memory to develop at its fastest pace.

Second, you must understand the basic mechanics of position play so that your brain has the fuel it needs to make the adjustments. The two major factors that determine the success of your position play are cue ball speed and English. By far speed is the most critical for the beginner to learn. In fact, we urge you to first learn how well you can play position with no English at all. Use only cue ball speed to move around the table for the next shot. This will allow you to learn the "natural" routes the cue ball takes. Once you have a good feeling for these natural paths, you can comfortably begin to alter them with English. Obviously, trying to alter the natural paths before you know where they are makes little sense and can harm your progress.

Speed control is one of those basic skills that even the best players in the world constantly work to improve. The fastest way to hone it is through drills. Again, the repetitiveness of the drills allows your muscle memory to develop quickly. Striking the cue ball in the center is another key element to the game. In the following speed drill, you are going to send the cue ball up and down the table with natural roll. We call it "natural roll" because you hit the cue ball in the center and by the time it reaches the rail it has no English and is just rolling naturally. If your aim is off and you are not hitting the cue ball in the center, then you are not making the same shot every time and your results will be inconsistent. If this happens, move your bridge hand closer to the cue ball and make sure you are hitting in the center. If the cue ball does not come straight back at you off of the rail (on a level table) then you are not hitting the center of the cue ball.

The idea of this first drill is to execute a proper "lag" shot. We have to do this at the beginning of each tournament match, so it is a great shot to pick up early and it teaches great speed control. As diagrammed in Figure 7.4, just place the cue ball anywhere along the head string and drive it straight away so that

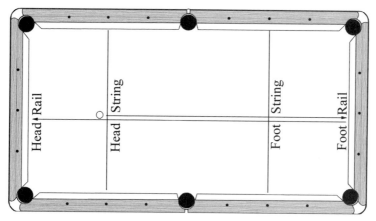

**Figure 7.4** *The lag drill.*

it goes down to the foot rail and rebounds right back toward you. Ideally it will come to a rest just as it touches the head cushion and you will have the perfect lag.

More than likely, however, you will come up either short or long. Notice exactly where it finishes and tell yourself whether you stroked too firmly or not firmly enough. Then imagine the successful shot again in your mind and give it another try. That marvelous brain of yours will adjust the arm speed and this next shot will be closer. As long as you are enjoying yourself, taking notice of whether the shot comes up short or long, and revisualizing prior to taking each shot, you will learn the shot quickly.

Once you can shoot this shot five times in a row and leave the cue ball between the rail and the first diamond, then you are ready to expand the drill. Now shoot the shot the same way but have it come off of the foot rail and rebound only to the first diamond. Then do it until it rebounds to the second diamond and then to the third and so on until you can leave the cue ball at any of these planes whenever you desire with only one diamond of slop on either side. (See Figure 7.5.)

To fine-tune your positional speed control, add an object ball. Set up the next shot as shown in Figure 7.6. The shot itself should be easy, just a simple cut into the closest corner. But the

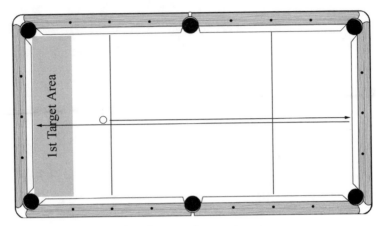

**Figure 7.5** *Land in the one diamond area.*

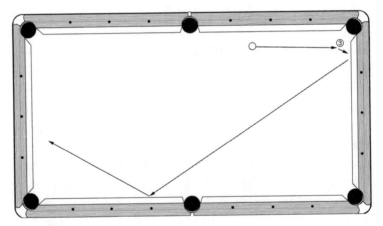

**Figure 7.6** *Speed control off of a shot.*

idea is to make the ball and then come two rails to get back down to the head rail. Again, once you can nestle the cue ball onto that cushion, start varying the shot by leaving the cue ball first one diamond up from the head rail, then two back, then three back, and so on down the table. All of this information gets programmed into your beautiful brain without any strain on your part. As your eyes see it happen, the adjustments will be made. One great aspect of this drill is that you must cut the object ball very thinly to hit the two rails as described. You can hit the object ball very full and make the shot, but that will alter the path of the cue ball so that it must go three rails instead of two to get back to the head rail. If you do these drills, you will improve as a matter of course.

These drills teach a very important point about the game. Quite often there are several aiming points that you can use to make the shot, but only one that will give you the position path you need to get to the next shot. File that information away in the "This is important!" part of your brain.

Before you go any further in this book, take this newfound knowledge and play for a few weeks, becoming more comfortable moving your cue, making balls, and controlling the speed of the cue ball. Once you are comfortable getting around a rack of 9-Ball, then come back and pick up at Chapter 8. We are about to tackle the subject of English, but there is definitely a wrong time to enter this territory. First you must be comfortable with the basics of stance, bridge, grip, stroke, shot-making, and speed control.

Once you are comfortable with those basics, adding a working knowledge of English to your game will take you to the next level. But you cannot get to this rung on the ladder if the ones beneath are still slippery. Be patient and give yourself time to become comfortable with the cue before taking on English. So put your bookmark here and go have some fun on the tables!

# 8

# English

*That's where the amateurs are different. They don't spin the*
*ball. They're afraid to leave the center of the cue ball.*

—EARL STRICKLAND

*E*nglish is defined as striking the cue ball either to the left or right of center. Topspin and draw (hitting above or beneath the center) also affect the path of the cue ball, but these are not technically "English." The way to remember the difference is that topspin and draw affect the path of the cue ball primarily after it strikes the object ball, while left and right English have little effect until the cue ball touches a rail.

A cue ball hit on the right side will spin in that direction. When it then contacts a rail, the friction of the spinning ball causes it to spin off the rail to the right. Conversely, if struck on the left-hand side, the cue ball will spin off a rail to the left.

A cue ball struck above center will contain energy in the form of topspin, which remains after contacting the object ball and continues to drive it in the direction it was moving before contact. A cue ball struck below center, with draw, will contain energy that draws it back toward the shooter after contact with the object ball.

The reason you will see pros on TV move the cue ball around the table seemingly at will, from precise point to precise point, is because they are skilled at predicting the path of the cue ball and altering that path as required with speed and English. Look at the shot diagrammed in Figure 8.1. If you hit the cue ball with no English at all, it will strike the rail at "A" and then rebound across the table dangerously close to a scratch. But if you hit it with right-hand (3-o'clock) English, it will still strike the rail at "A" and then the English will kick in and send it well wide of the scratch.

Or, you can draw the cue ball away from the 3-ball and not touch the side rail at all or use topspin to drive into the rail early,

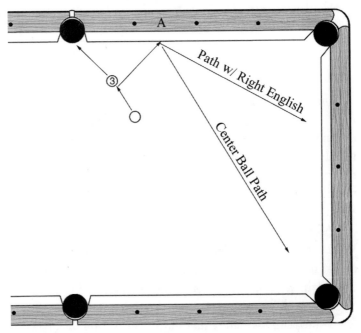

**Figure 8.1** *Using English to avoid a potential scratch.*

as shown in Figure 8.2. So while the sidespin did not affect the path of the cue ball off of the object ball, the topspin and draw most certainly did. And that is the primary difference between topspin, bottom spin, and sidespin. Sidespin is used to alter the path of the cue ball off of the rails while topspin and bottom spin are used to alter the path off of the object ball. Additionally, you can combine topspin or bottom spin with sidespin to get whatever effect it is you desire.

The key to mastering the effects of sidespin involves "clocking" the cue ball. Draw an imaginary clock face on the cue ball and refer to the numbers on the clock as your aiming points. Take the same shot with right-hand English that we have worked with before. Make certain as you go through this exercise that you are not accidentally using any topspin or bottom spin, just pure 3-o'clock sidespin. We know from before that no

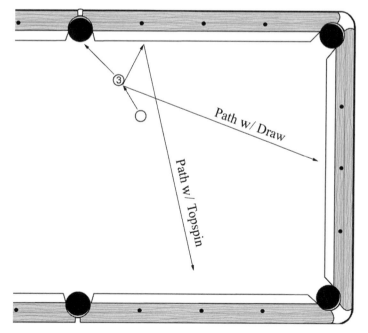

**Figure 8.2** *Shot with draw or topspin.*

spin sends it into the dump for a scratch. But, as shown in Figure 8.3, just half a cue tip of right sends it to a safe point. A full cue tip sends it along yet another track, while a tip and a half sends it still farther away from the hole. Which method you decide to use to avoid scratching is determined by the path you want the cue ball to take to get in position for the next shot.

Learn to get a feel for how much angle you get off of this shot at each position of the cue tip. Your subconscious can apply this information to many different shots and this all becomes a part of trusting your visualization and then executing. Once you feed all the coordinates into your brain, you just have to trust it to do its work and to keep refining itself until your skills become more and more accurate and dependable. There are more drills for perfecting your English play in Chapter 13. Practice them until the mystery of English is removed.

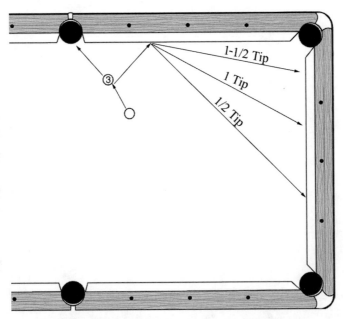

**Figure 8.3** *More English equals more angle.*

Let's delve a little deeper into the effects of topspin and draw. We have shown how their effect on the cue ball when coming off the object ball is priceless. Normally, the cue ball will always leave the object ball along the tangent line, a line drawn 90 degrees off the line of contact with the object ball. Indeed, this tangent line is the basis for predicting the paths of all colliding balls. The object ball always leaves along the path of contact, shown in the diagram in Figure 8.4 where the cue ball was shot from position "A." As you can see, the contacting ball (usually the cue ball) always departs the scene along the tangent line.

Knowing the cue ball will always leave the scene of the collision along the tangent line is of great help to your brain when it comes to aiming. If the eyes see the cue ball leaving the object ball along a line other than the tangent line, then the brain knows that the aim was off and can correct accordingly. You need not miss a shot for your aim to be off. Pockets are twice as large as object balls, so you can be a full ball-width off in aim and still make some shots. The goal is to drive the ball to the exact point at the rear of the pocket that you intended.

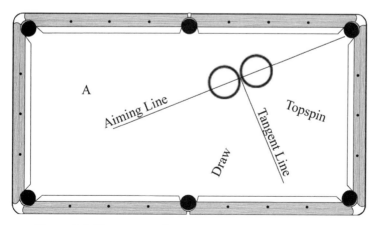

**Figure 8.4** The tangent line.

If neither topspin nor bottom spin is affecting the cue ball when it makes contact with the object ball, it will leave the contact point along the tangent line and continue to travel along that line until its course is altered by a collision with another ball or a rail. But we can alter this tangent-line path with topspin or draw, as previously shown in Figure 8.2. The paths the cue ball can be made to assume are shown and properly labeled. Topspin will drive the cue ball forward of the tangent line, while draw will pull the cue ball back away from the tangent line. You can generate milder or more acute angles of deviation by applying more or less topspin or draw.

These alterations are mind-numbing in what they can do as far as moving that cue ball exactly where you want it to go. But when you toss in a little sidespin—which we now know will kick in when the cue ball hits a rail—suddenly there is almost no spot on the table that you cannot drive the cue ball into with a little work! This is the *power* of the great pool player, and it is the rock upon which champions stand. Speed control and English control combined with topspin and bottom spin are all of the positional weapons at your command, and it is the mastery of these that will determine your place in the pecking order of the game.

Keep in mind that cue speed affects anything that you do to the cue ball. Hitting a shot firmly increases the application of topspin or bottom spin, so a ball will travel farther along the path dictated by the topspin or bottom spin when struck more firmly. But sidespin reacts in just the opposite manner. The more gently a ball is struck, the greater the effect of the English on the rail since the ball spends more time on the rail when hit slowly than when pounded. In time this will all become part of your subconscious computer, and your cue tip will go to the right spot on the ball and your arm will deliver the correct stroke speed.

You should also realize that the amount of English you can apply, that is the distance away from center that you can strike the cue ball, is a direct result of how well you stroke combined with the friction generated by a well-groomed tip. You should begin your experiments with English by applying no more than a half tip at a time. Get comfortable with this amount before going on to the extremes. Pros can hit way out on the edge of the ball without mis-cueing, but their tips are perfect, nickel-rounded shapes with the leather carefully roughened to accept chalk and they are stroking the ball very well. (See Figure 8.5.) Crawl before you jump into a marathon, or you will only frustrate yourself.

If you work the drills in Chapter 13 and allow yourself to become proficient at them, you will become an awesome pool player. Accept the fact the game requires that you master a few basic physical movements and after that the game is largely mental. This is a game of confidence born of practice, knowledge, and experience. Many players have the knowledge required to

**Figure 8.5** *Pros such as Karen Corr can use edge English because of their clean strokes.*

be great. The difference is in the few players who will devote themselves to the practice necessary to become dependable with their basic shot skills.

English is one of the most advanced topics of the game and cannot be mastered quickly. The amount of time you spend in dedicated practice will correlate directly with how quickly you become comfortable with sidespin. This is one area of the game that you will continue to refine as long as you play. It is an area that will evolve naturally, and you should not attempt to rush the process. If you want to get better faster than your friends, then spend more time practicing than they do. The application of English and your comfort in using it will increase with each session at the table.

Again, English is a very individual aspect of the game. Some players constantly preach, as multiple World Champion Willie Mosconi did, that center ball is king and speed control alone is key to position. Earl Strickland, on the other hand, has been quoted as saying that the biggest weakness he sees in amateurs is that "they don't spin the ball enough; they're afraid of English." What is right for either of them is not necessarily right for you. Develop your own style, the one that makes you most comfortable, and thrive there.

# 9

# Bank Shots

*I don't know why he thinks he's a banks player. That's not banks. You're not playing banks till you're hitting 'em with enough juice that they bend around other balls after they come off the rail.*

—JOHN BRUMBACK

The bank shot is one that many players find intimidating. Relax. Learn a few basics, and you will find the banks open up for you and reward you with riches of pocketed balls. Not only is the bank required to get out of safeties and unfavorable positions, it also gives you another positional tool, one that can be used to navigate yourself profitably around the table.

First, let's understand the rails. Many people believe that the angle the ball rebounds from a rail is the mirror opposite of the angle that the ball struck the rail. That is, that the angle of incidence is equal to the angle of rebound—45 degrees in, 45 degrees out. Well, almost. That equal-angle stuff works fine on light beams coming off of perfectly polished mirrors, but those table rails are imperfect and they differ slightly from table to table. Figures 9.1 and 9.2 show what we mean.

The diagram in Figure 9.1 is the one you see most often. It shows that the bank shot consists of two equal angles. The angle into the rail is equal to the angle off of the rail. This would be handy if it was true, but it simply is not. You see, the rails have a "deadening" affect on angles. Balls will come off of the rails at slightly less of an angle than they went into the rail. Figure 9.2 is more accurate.

As you can see, the rail "shortened" the rebound angle and the ball missed the intended target pocket. This is critical knowledge. Realizing this makes it much easier to formulate the correct angle for bank shots and avoid years of frustration believing in the incorrect assumption that the angle in equals the angle out. Remove the cue ball entirely and stroke the object ball directly into the rail to obtain an elementary feel for the effect of the bank.

To make the beginning shot with no English, aim the object ball just to the left of the middle diamond. How much depends on the individual table. You must judge a table before you begin playing upon it to determine the amount of adjustment required. But the basic idea is to hit the previous shot as a test

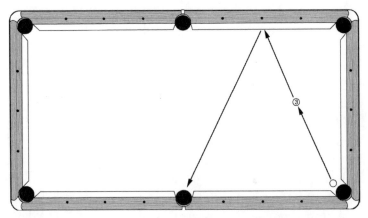

**Figure 9.1** *The ideal: a bank shot with two equal angles.*

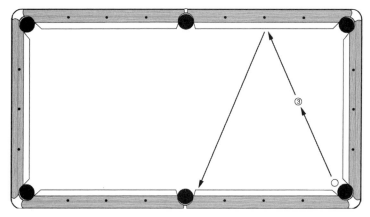

**Figure 9.2** *In reality, a bank shot comes off the rail at an angle that is slightly less than the original angle.*

before you begin playing. Hit it with medium speed and no English (center ball). See how far short of the pocket it falls, and then adjust your aiming point by about two-thirds of that amount. Then hit another test shot. Adjust again for any error, and you should be able to pocket that ball time after time. (See Figure 9.3.)

Now that you know the amount of adjustment for a bank shot that is full rail wide, you can make other simple adjustments. For example, when playing a bank shot that is a half-rail in width, you should adjust for an error that is one-half that of the previous shot. All of your banks can be adjusted properly off of the single test shot just described according to the amount of rail they involve.

While most banks shots are not straight-on as was the previous one, they must be shot as if they are. To make the required adjustments for aiming the off-angle bank shots, simply use your imagination to "straighten" the shot. Determine where a cue ball would strike the object ball if it were straight-on, and then cut the object ball accordingly to achieve that effect. Look at Figure 9.4.

In this shot the cue ball and object ball do not lie conveniently along the line of travel required to make the shot. Strik-

**Figure 9.3** *Just relax and aim the shot.*

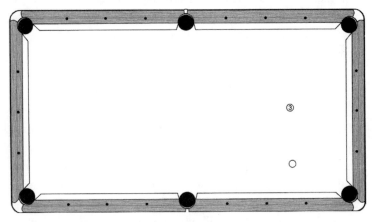

**Figure 9.4** *The cue ball and object ball are not conveniently lined up.*

ing the 3-ball straight-on will result in it coming back off the rail and striking the cue ball again, falling nowhere near the desired side pocket. So you must "move" the cue ball over in your mind to see where you must make contact, as in Figure 9.5.

The X lies on the line that bisects the aiming point on the object ball. Were the cue ball sitting where the X is, then a straight-on shot would complete the shot successfully. So by cutting the 3-ball at that point, we hit the shot just as if we were lined up straight-on to it.

This is true of all bank shots. Find the aiming point on the object ball that lines up with a straight-on bank shot and you have the key to making the shot.

Sometimes, however, the aiming point is at a point on the ball where striking it could result in a scratch or being helplessly out of position for the next shot. This is where you must be able to change the aiming point in order to move the cue ball to a desirable place on the table for the next shot. There are two ways (often used in combination) to alter the aiming point. Figure 9.6 illustrates the use of stroke speed.

Again, you should shoot bank shots with medium speed. If you hit the shots very firmly, they will "shorten up" coming

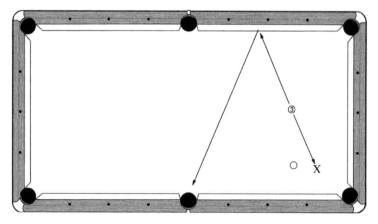

**Figure 9.5** *Move the cue ball over in your mind to see where to make contact.*

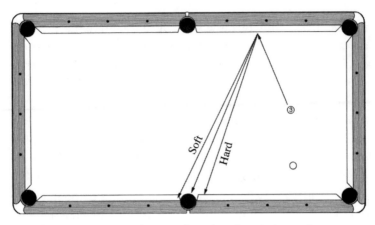

**Figure 9.6** *Use stroke speed to alter the aiming point.*

off of the rail and, as a result, come up short of the original target. If you hit them softly, the angle will lengthen out slightly and your target area will extend away from you.

Use this knowledge to change the contact point on the object ball slightly. That is, you can hit the 3-ball a little more on the right side and still make the shot in the side pocket if you hit the ball more firmly. Conversely, you can hit the 3-ball softly a little more on the left and still make the shot as that angle will be lengthened for you. Also, if you strike the shot with topspin, the object ball will develop a small amount of draw and this will shorten the angle. Hitting the shot with draw, conversely, will slightly lengthen the angle. It does this through the "gear effect" in which spinning billiard balls react to one another like gears— a ball spinning to the left will cause any ball it collides with to spin to the right and vice versa.

But stroke speed or topspin or bottom spin alone often will not alter the angle enough for you. Usually you will need to "twist" the object ball off of the rail by using English. With English you can "throw" the object ball a considerable distance, and by combining English with stroke speed you can change where the cue ball winds up after the shot while still making the shot.

When you throw in topspin and draw, you can command the cue ball to almost any place on the table after the shot is made. Bank shots, with this knowledge, do not limit position play at all and may in fact improve your ability to get where you need to be for the next shot. Figure 9.7 illustrates how English affects the course of the ball.

What you should notice first is that we altered the course of the ball considerably by applying English to the shot. This is because the English transfers from the cue ball to the object ball. So a cue ball struck with the right English will impart (through the gear effect) left English to the object ball. A cue ball striking the rail while carrying left English will spin to the left off of the rail, thereby lengthening the shot angle.

The opposite is true of a cue ball struck with left English. The right-hand spin of the object ball that results will shorten the angle off of the rail.

By practicing the bank shot using a combination of speed and English, you will find that the shot is a lot easier to control than you may have thought. But always remember that while you must develop proficiency at bank shots, they are always more difficult than cut shots. This is true for two reasons: you are not aiming directly at the pocket and the condition of the

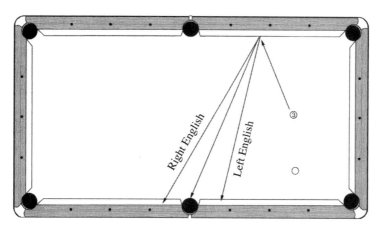

**Figure 9.7** *The effects of English.*

rails introduces variables. As a result, pros play to get positions on cut shots, not banks.

Always consider the variables thrown in by the equipment on which you are playing. High-quality tables, such as the Brunswick Gold Crown tournament table, will give consistent rail-to-rail performance while bargain-brand tables may vary considerably.

# 10

# ● Safety Play ●

*I learned real fast you gotta be more than a shot-maker. Everybody out here is a shot-maker. What wins when shot-making won't is being able to put the other guy in jail. Tie him up so bad he can't make a good hit, and you'll usually win the game. Ball in hand is tough to lose from.*

—CORY DEUEL

When you first take up pocket billiards, it is all about having fun and making balls. But at some point the competitor in you will begin to stretch and that will no longer be enough. Now you will have to begin to win consistently. It is then that you will realize that between two players of equal ability, the winner is most often the player making the fewest mistakes.

One of the most common mistakes in novice-level pool is trying to make a shot where there is no shot to be made or when no positional advantage is possible. It is for these instances that you will learn the beauty of a well-timed and executed safety. Considered by many to be a defensive move since no balls are usually falling, safeties are actually one of the most powerful offensive weapons in the game. To paraphrase actor and humorist Will Rogers, "playing a safety is a lot like saying 'good doggie' until you can find a rock!"

For this discussion to be the most concise, assume that we are talking about 9-Ball. Safeties are played in all pocket billiard games, but 9-Ball is where you will see them used on television. So we will use that format as our example.

The object of the game of 9-Ball is *not* to break the balls and then run all the balls on the table until you sink the 9-ball. It is much more simple than that. The object is just to sink the 9. Nothing else matters. If I do a beautiful job of breaking the rack and running all the balls except the 9 and my opponent comes to the table with a shot and makes the 9, I lose. All of that breaking and making balls was a waste of time because I lost control of the table at the wrong moment. I cost myself the game by not sinking the 9-ball.

That is the key to the game. You must *always* control the table. It is your goal to never let your opponent have control. If you get into a situation where you cannot make a shot and get position for the next shot, it is time to play a safety. (See Figure 10.1.) As with all shots, you should define for yourself a clear-cut objective when playing safeties. Many players tend to "let up" when it comes to

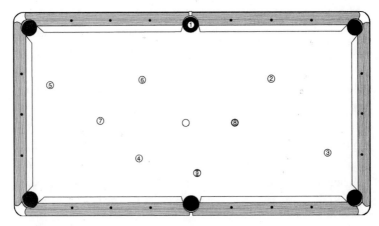

**Figure 10.1** *No need for safeties here!*

safeties because they are unhappy about having to turn over the table. But safeties are generally more difficult to execute than pocketing shots since excellent speed control must be exercised over both the cue ball and the object ball. This is no time to relax!

The goal of safety play is quite simple: deny your opponent any opportunity to either begin making balls or to play a return safety that puts you in a tough situation. Ideally, your opponent will not even be able to hit the object ball and will wind up committing a foul that gives you ball in hand and a great chance to win. That is exactly what good safeties can do for you. They can deliver you from a hopeless situation and put your opponent there instead. Let's take a look at the example in Figure 10.2. Here you broke the balls and the 3-ball fell and left you a shot on the 1-ball. The 2-ball is open and you can get there easily from the 1-ball. But the 4-ball is tucked in behind the 5 and there is no good shot at making it in the corner. You could try banking it across the table, but that is risky because if you miss, your opponent gets to come to the table with only six balls on it. Being a hero in this situation and uncorking a bank may well cost you the game. If you are playing someone who runs racks, that single error could cost you a number of games. Remember the three *D*s of pool: Don't Do Dumb. Figure 10.2 shows a perfect chance to play a safety and win the game.

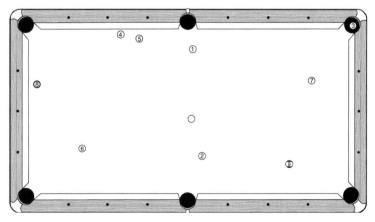

**Figure 10.2** *Think about safeties early in the game.*

First, play the 1-ball and 2-ball in their respective side pockets and leave the cue ball in the middle of the table as shown in the first diagram in Figure 10.3. Then just hit the 4-ball with a stop shot and send it three rails! Look at the second diagram in Figure 10.3. to see the marvelous thing that happens when you do this. First, you get to go sit down while your opponent comes to the table with a real migraine of a situation because he can't hit the ball. He has to figure out a way to kick into the 4-ball, make a good hit, and then leave you without a shot, which is no easy task.

So, in one simple move, you went from the underdog position of being a player faced with a tough shot to the "favorite-to-win" position of being the player who is about to possibly get ball in hand or at least a shot on the ball. And with only a shot on the ball you have retained control of the table and can choose to play yet another safety if you so desire. If you can make him foul three times in a row, you win the game. And if you keep your opponents kicking, you will frustrate them and cause them to take unnecessary chances that can pay off in your favor.

You must develop a strong safety strategy for your game to step up to the next level. There are a tremendous number of advantages to doing so. One major component is the importance of confidence and the mental game in billiards. When someone refuses to give you control of the table and instead keeps you kicking and scrambling, it is very tough to maintain that positive mental attitude (PMA).

One of the basic tenets of pool is that if your options include either going for the shot or playing a safety, ask yourself which is the tougher shot to complete. If you have an 80 percent chance of completing the safety but only a 25 percent chance of making the shot, then you should play the odds and go for the safety. But if the odds are close to even, then go for the shot. Players are often seen failing at really tough safeties when there was a shot available that they might have made. If you are going to

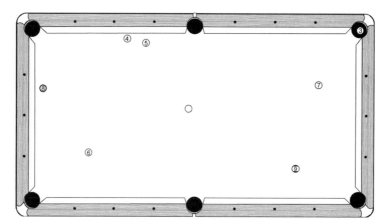

**Figure 10.3a** *A great safety setup.*

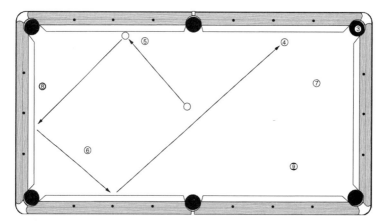

**Figure 10.3b**

give up the table in a favorable situation for the other guy, it is better to go down firing than ducking. Let him know that you are not afraid of the tough shots and it further limits what he can do against you.

Safety situations often arise when you get into a troublesome situation as a result of the break. This is part of the initial rack planning that you must do after every break. You must plan the table and see if you can win the game by staying at the table, making every ball in order, and running out. Often there will be a cluster of balls or blocking balls or impossible shots from which to gain position that mean a run-out is unfeasible. If you are not going to run out, then you must pick a ball in the rack from which to play safe. Further, you should remember that the best safeties are those that result in your coming back to the table with an opportunity to win.

Even if your initial plan is to run out, there are bad things that happen during play that cause the plan to be reformulated and to include safeties. You might overrun or come up short on your position and not have the shot on the next ball that you need. Suddenly, your plan changes to include a safety! As you improve your level of play, how often your plan changes during a rack will become a touchstone of your ability. Surprise safeties are particularly common in the novice class.

Take a look at the layout in Figure 10.4. The 1-ball went in on the break and you have a shot on the 2-, the 3-, and the 4-ball. But that 5 is tucked right up under the wing of the 8-ball, and there is no pocket that ball will fall into on purpose. So you have to run all the way down there and then play a safety unless you can break up the friendship between the 5-ball and the 8-ball before you get there.

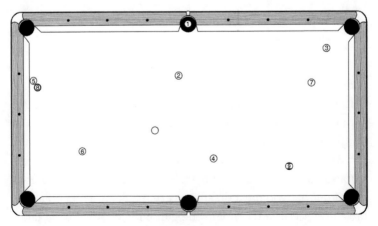

*Figure 10.4 See a safety coming?*

This is a situation where preventing your opponent from hitting the object ball is unlikely. You do not have a lot of balls left out there to hide behind. So the idea is to leave him tough. Give him a shot that all he can do is hit and hope. The two key factors in leaving someone tough are distance and angle. Leave the object ball as far away from the cue ball as you possibly can while also leaving as tough an angle on the ball as possible. In our example in Figure 10.5, we want to leave the cue ball in the area shown after the 4-ball so we can barely brush the edge of the 5 and send the cue ball at least two rails and 9 feet away, maybe even coming to rest behind the 9-ball.

If you play the shot as we have shown here, you will likely maintain control of the table and frustrate your opponent. Be careful not to hit too much of that 5-ball or it will bounce off the 8-ball and come right out in front of the corner pocket. If you have not gotten behind the 9-ball, the other guy will take your safety and slap you firmly with your own creation. Remember to concentrate on the shot, aim to just nip the 5-ball so that hardly any energy gets transferred from the cue ball to move the 5 around, and all is well. Lapse into laziness and hit this one even a hair too full and you could be racking the next game instead of breaking.

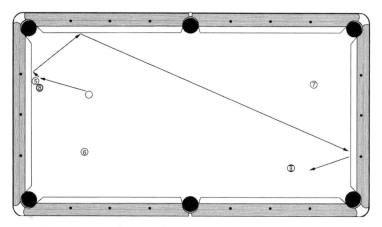

**Figure 10.5** *A fine result.*

The situation in Figure 10.6 is one of the most common ones that you will encounter. Your shot is on the 5-ball, but it is blocked from the pocket by the 7-ball and the 8-ball. The key is to see this one ahead of time and plan to get into position for the 5-ball so that you can hit a stop shot (in which the cue ball stops where it contacts the 5-ball), replace the 5 with the cue, and send the 5 to the other side of the 7-ball for a safety. This isn't the greatest safety in the world because your opponent has an easy kick (striking the rail with the cue ball prior to hitting the object ball) to make a good hit. But at least he is kicking, and you then have the opportunity to come to the table with a shot that you can make.

Let's take a look at another common situation in Figure 10.7a. Here you can see the 1-ball, but the shot is just too tough in relation to the safety. The only shot option is to bank the ball up table for the corner. This shot doesn't have the greatest odds in the world. The situation is intensified by the position of the 2-ball. Even if you make the bank on the 1-ball, it is almost impossible to get back for the next shot. But the safety is simple. Just carom the cue ball off the 1-ball, sending it over to squat behind that little cluster, as shown in Figure 10.7b. Once

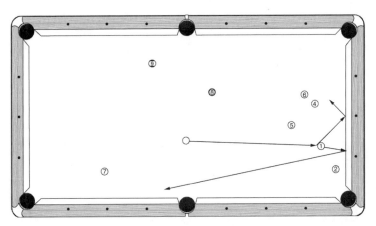

**Figure 10.6** *A common situation calling for a safety.*

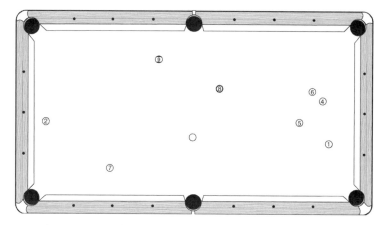

**Figure 10.7a** *The safety carries better odds and it works well.*

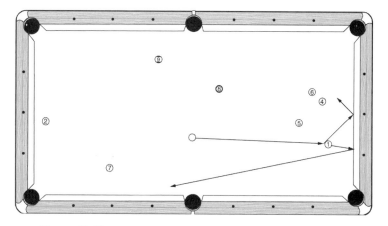

**Figure 10.7b**

again you have not only transferred a problem over to your opponent, you have also made it worse! Good job.

Look for the very fortunate two-way variation on this shot. Sometimes you can go for the bank shot and play safe at the same time. If you bank the 1-ball here, the cue ball will be in-line to make the 2-ball. But if you miss the bank, the cue ball is behind that cluster and no shot is available. This is just another example of keeping all of the control on your side of the room.

There are countless variations and situations that involve safety play. Safeties are another very sharp arrow in your quiver. But like any other aspect of the game, they must be practiced until you are comfortable executing them—or they will turn against you if you fail to complete them correctly. Do your drills and master the safeties that come up time and time again. Learning these will teach you to recognize others and give you the skills required to execute a wide range of different shots.

# 11

# The Coin-Operated
## ● Table ●

*You can't get careless on the small table. One little lapse and
you roll up behind a crowd and give the game away.*

—DAVID MATLOCK

Pool is played on three common sizes of tables. The smallest
of these is the coin-operated table, often found in taverns or
rooms of limited size. (See Figure 11.1.) These tables are usually 3½ feet wide by 7 feet long. The other two popular sizes
are the 8-foot table and the 9-foot table, both of which are more
often found in private homes and billiard rooms.

Many people assume that since the coin-operated table is
the smallest, it is the easiest to learn to play well on. Analyze this
a moment and you might find the devil in the details. A 3½-by-
7-foot bar table has a rail-to-rail surface of 38 inches by 76
inches. An 8-foot model is 44 inches by 88 inches and a 9-footer
is 50 inches by 100 inches. So that gives tables of 2,888 square
inches, 3,872 square inches, and 5,000 square inches. So, while

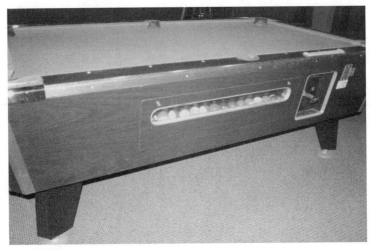

**Figure 11.1** *The coin-operated table is the smallest of the billiard tables.*

a 9-foot table is only about 25 percent longer and wider than a coin-operated table, it has nearly double the surface playing area!

All of which means that playing position on a small table calls for more precision than on a big track. The balls are the same size on all tables, so they are much bigger "blockers" on the small table. In addition, the windows you must move the cue ball through to get position are much tighter on the smaller surface. There are other factors that make life on the little guys tougher than one might first imagine. For instance, the cushions on a coin-operated version react differently than on the big tables, the pockets are cut differently, and the table is easier to move out of position accidentally, possibly making it unlevel. Plus, these tables as a group are not maintained as carefully by their owners as are the larger tables that carry a larger initial investment to protect. Bank shots get downright tricky when the rail rebounds at a different angle on one side of the table than it does on another side.

So, let's see what we have so far—a tighter playing surface, inconsistent conditions, and maybe an unlevel table. Now let's add in the final component—the coin-operated table cue ball.

Since most of these tables rely on the cue ball being a different weight or size from the object balls in order to tell it apart and send it back out for play after a scratch, the cue ball here plays a lot differently than on standard tables. Technology is now beginning to change this, but for now most small track players are stuck with a ball that has a metal core and is heavy. This means that the ball is easy to make follow a shot but difficult to draw because of the relative mass of the two colliding balls. Since the cue ball is heavier than the object ball, the cue ball tends to roll through the plane of the object ball and just keep going. To draw this monster you have to overdo it, putting enough backspin on the ball to overcome the inertial weight differences of the balls. That difference in weight is considerable in terms of percentage.

This brings us to some rules for small table play. For one, since it is easier to overshoot or undershoot your target area, avoid playing position for the side pockets whenever possible. This becomes clear when you realize that if you are a little short or long playing position for a corner pocket, you can still get down to the rest of the table. But if you overshoot a side pocket, the cue ball winds up headed in the wrong direction for the next shot. Most great coin-op table players pretend there are no side pockets on the table.

The diagrams in Figures 11.2 and 11.3 show this strategy clearly. In both we have drawn in the "line of position" for you. This is the line that intersects both the center of the object ball and the center of the intended target pocket. Generally speaking, when you make a plan for running the table, you always tell yourself which side of that line you must be on in order to get to the next shot. But as you can see, you can overshoot the line to either side when going for the corner shot and the cue ball will still be headed down toward the 3-ball after the 2-ball is pocketed.

If you attempt to play the same ball in the side pocket and overshoot your position on that shot, then the cue ball is headed in the wrong direction to easily get to the 3-ball. This confuses

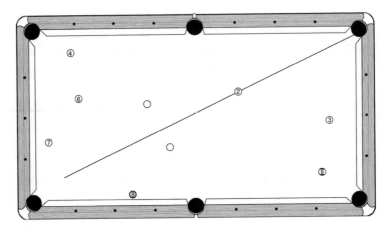

*Figure 11.2* *A little room for error.*

a lot of people, but it need not disturb you. Just resolve to play for the corners whenever possible, and you will make the job of running out a lot easier.

The next step is to try to play position so that you can use follow to get to the next shot. When you're playing in a situation where draw is tough and follow is easy, well, *follow* the path of least resistance.

An advantage to the brutish cue ball that comes with the coin-operated tables is the break shot. Essentially, it's like driv-

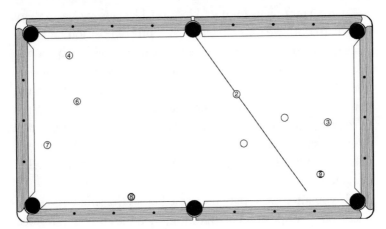

*Figure 11.3* *Side pockets are tricky.*

ing a cannonball into a cluster of grapeshot and you can really scatter them. (**Important tip:** Never use an expensive cue on the break shot as it flattens the tip and damages the ferrule and shaft. This is particularly true on the coin-op box with the heavier cue ball.) Develop a monster break and you can nearly guarantee your chance of staying at the table after the break. The break shot of choice varies from game to game and player to player, but in 9-Ball try the cut break. Instead of hitting the 1-ball square on the face, try just hitting off to one side and letting the cue ball fly to the rails and back into the rack again. This double whammy with the big ball can get an awful lot of action stirred up, and nothing widens the eyes of a foe like three balls going in on the snap. You'll have them reaching for their wallet before they screw their stick together.

When playing on a coin-op table, knowledge is vital. Before ever beginning to play, check the level of the table and the condition of the rails. Stand at one end of the table and drop a ball from about 4 inches up so that it hits the edge of the rail and is sent down the table. (See Figure 11.4.) This allows you to send it down table in a straight line without the inevitable English applied by the arm and hand. Watch for and note any table drift. Do the same thing from the side rails across the width of the table. If the table is rolling off enough, you can just lag a ball toward a corner or even side pocket and gravity will roll it right on in there. Anyone who has played this game for a while has seen a small table situation where an object ball rolled around a blocking ball and gravity fed it right down into the pocket. This is handy knowledge to have, particularly if your opponent hasn't bothered to notice.

As for the rails, you need to know if they are consistent. Good or bad doesn't matter nearly as much as consistency. If all the rails are coming up short, you can just adjust your bank and kick shots to compensate. But if one rail is short and another is long, the only option you have is to put away your banks and kicks and start sharpening those cuts. To check the rails, take any ball in your hand and toss it against the rail so it rebounds

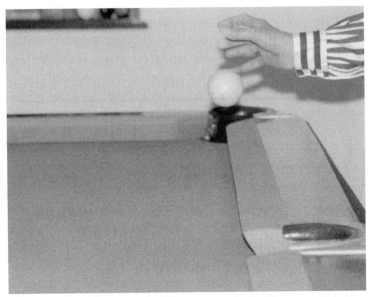

**Figure 11.4** *Make sure you're on the level by dropping a ball so it hits a rail and then watching it roll down the table.*

back out across the table into your hand, as shown in Figure 11.5. As you do this, listen carefully. If the rail is inconsistent, you will hear different sounds at different points. If you get the same noise everywhere the cue ball hits the rails, the rails are consistent and you can bank and kick away to your heart's content.

Let's assume that the rails are consistent and the table is level. One advantage the learned player has on a coin-op table is that kicks are easier. Again, because there are fewer square inches on the bar box, the shots are shorter, and short kicks are much easier than long kicks—which means that safety play on the little guys can be a little tougher. For this reason most people tend to play a bit more aggressively on them than on the large tables. In other words, shift your gearing toward the shots a little and away from the safeties. Since the table is smaller, shots are somewhat easier to complete and safeties are easier for your opponent to escape. Logic demands that you play more aggressively and not try to duck as often as you would on the bigger tables.

**Figure 11.5** *Check each rail by tossing a ball against it and listening for a consistent sound.*

Here's another very important tip: On all tables, but especially on the smaller ones, set the table up to your liking by playing any required safeties early in the rack. You have more blocking balls out there to hide behind early on in the game than you do later, so use this to your advantage and hide early if indeed you must hide. When you watch a coin-op expert play, you will see him or her move the balls around on the table while playing safe early and then run out once the table has been arranged in such a fashion that this is possible. It is a thinking player's game. If you only make a few balls and then turn over the table to the other guy, you are going to become very familiar with losing.

Finally, the coin-op table has one major drawback for someone just learning the game—it doesn't allow you to "let your stroke out" and shoot with a free, loose, and powerful arm. Since the table is smaller, you are using less power to drive the balls around the table. It is far easier to learn the game on a bigger table so that you can use your full stroke. This is similar to golf where it is difficult to learn the game by only playing par 3 courses. It will be easier for you to progress if you begin on the big tables and develop a long, smooth stroke before going to the small tables. You can always "choke up" on your stroke, but it is more difficult to learn to play that way first and then try to import and alter that style for the larger surfaces.

# 12

# A Winning Attitude

*He thinks he can win and sometimes that's enough.*

—Tony Robles

We have already spoken briefly about the importance of the mental game in pocket billiards. Your initial exposure to the game will be dominated by learning and becoming comfortable with the basic mechanics, such as stance, grip, and stroke. But your true initiation into the game doesn't come until you are through that gate and begin to think your way around the table.

This is when you will begin to appreciate the intricacies of pocket billiards. The chaos of the break shot provides a different layout for you to conquer each time you start a new rack. The geometry of the balls and the rails and the paths that are first imagined and then created to play position properly are a source of wonder to be explored for years. You may never see the same three-rail combination twice, but learning only one will help you play all of the rest of them.

At some point you will begin to develop instincts about the game. You will have made enough bank shots that you no longer need to carefully measure the angles. You will begin to "see" the banks, and your arm will begin to tell you when you are in-line with the shot. Your muscle memory will take over, and you will just know when to pull the trigger. When you first began playing billiards, you may have thought that the game is very similar to golf. Just another stick and ball. But as you play more, you will realize that it has much more the quality of chess. It is not you against the table after all; it is you against a foe. You can assault your opponents with shot-making or frustrate them with safety play. And you can combine the two in any fashion you so desire. You play different people different ways.

You read their body language at the table and the emotion in their face. If you can make them give up and get distracted by playing safeties, then that is how you beat them. If you are playing someone who does not get frustrated and can beat you at your own safety game, then you shoot a more offensive game plan, revolving around running the table. In most games there is also an unwritten law that if you are ahead on the score bead, you play like a lamb. If you are behind, you play like a lion. You will learn that if you are to lose it is always better to go down firing, at least you are giving yourself the chance to win.

You will soon learn that winners expect to win, and many losers expect to lose. When playing someone whom you know to be a better player, it is very tough to maintain a positive attitude about winning. That expectation of loss becomes a self-fulfilling prophecy and history continues to repeat. What you absolutely must train yourself to do is to realize that in the game of pool anything can happen and that you largely have control over your own fate.

Remember, the entire path to victory is paved with controlling the table. If you will map out a plan to win each game without turning the table over to your opponent, you can defeat anyone. But even more important is this basic rule: You must really enjoy winning. Learn to savor victory internally; let yourself feel good about each win. Avoid boastfulness and gloating, which are negatives for anyone. But enjoy winning, particularly over better players, as this self-reward will drive you to new playing heights.

You must develop your positive mental attitude (PMA) about winning, and you must have fun playing the game. The game is played almost exclusively in the subconscious, and the interaction between the subconscious and conscious mind is only smooth when you are relaxed, confident, and happy. Remember that you are never "telling" your arm what to do, you are simply providing it with a picture (an image) to follow and then trusting it to deliver a winning stroke. This makes even the physical aspect of the game mostly dependent upon the ability of the mind to communicate effectively with the arm.

Let's walk through the mental exercises involved in a game of pool. First you will determine the winner of the break by either lag or coin toss. Assume we won the break. Then the mental work begins. You first set a goal for your break shot. Since this is 9-Ball, you want to break the rack apart cleanly by hitting the 1-ball square on the nose and you want the cue ball to rebound back to somewhere near the center of the table.

Given that a ball goes down and you have a shot, then you must plan the table, as Steve does in Figure 12.1. Can you run out, or must you play a safety at some point? Are there clusters that must be broken up, or balls that need to be moved in order to be made? Can we accomplish this without giving up the table?

If so, then you must consider each shot individually. You must plan to make the ball and move to the right place on the table to make the next shot. Before you play every shot, you must reassure yourself that you will make the shot, visualize yourself making the shot, and then be confident that your arm will do what is required to make your mental image of the shot a reality.

As you can see, there is actually a lot more mental exercise occurring than physical and that is a fundamental of the game that nonplayers never grasp. If you are going to become a win-

*Figure 12.1* Remember to start each game with a plan just as Steve Mizerak does.

ner at this game, it will only be after you begin to think of yourself as a winner. Develop solid fundamentals and believe in your ability to deliver, as 1998 Player of the Year Francisco Bustamante does. (See Figure 12.2.) Play smart, play cool, and play like a winner to become one.

*Figure 12.2* Francisco Bustamante plays without doubts. So should you.

Finally, never let doubt creep into your game. When you miss, use the miss to calculate an adjustment for the next similar shot. Never let the miss cause you to doubt yourself. Everyone misses. The champions go on to win anyway.

Now go practice to win! The drills in Chapter 13 will provide you with the skill sets required to make you a winner. Work on these for an hour a day for the first year that you play and you will become a force in your local room. How quickly you advance will be a combination of practice time and attitude. Always play to win, play the odds properly on shot versus safety, and play with confidence and joy. The basics you have learned here can carry you for life. Enjoy!

# 13

# Drills for ● Perfection ●

*I'm lucky. I enjoy practicing.*

—NICK VARNER

The following drills are intended to help you hone your basic skills and progress rapidly to a level of control. Since these drills give you the repetition required to develop muscle memory, performing them for only a few minutes each day will improve your game more rapidly than hours of playing without practice. Simply choose a few to do each day and work on them before you play a game.

We suggest that you work on these drills in the order they are presented so that you graduate from one basic skill to another. Gaining pool skills is like stacking blocks, the upper ones rely on the proper positioning of the lower ones for their success.

Always keep in mind that you are seeking a smooth action in the stroke. Your backstroke should be slower than your forward stroke, and you should be relaxed and comfortable.

We will start you on a drill that is very simple—the lag drill. Do not be too hasty to leave this drill behind. It gives you great opportunity to practice all of your basics. Here you can hone your stance, grip, bridge, and stroke. Remain with this one drill until you are comfortable executing the shot. Note that we said *comfortable*, not *skilled*. Your skills will come in due course. Your first goal is to develop basics and repeat them until you are comfortable at the table. You will never be consistent until you are comfortable and confident. Consistency is the hallmark of every champion.

Finally, please remember to have fun. After all, this is a *game!*

## Lag Drill

This is the most basic of all drills. Place the cue ball on the head spot and drive it to the end rail with enough speed for it to rebound as closely as possible to the head rail. (See Figure 13.1.)

This simple drill is valuable because it allows you to work on all of your basics without the complications injected by the object ball. While shooting this, strive to bring the cue ball

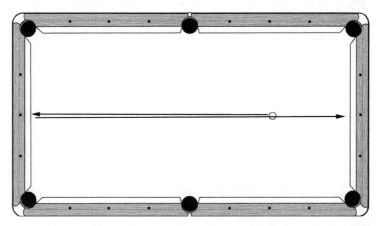

**Figure 13.1** Lag Drill.

back across the spot from which it began. If you can do this reliably, you know that you are hitting the cue ball where you intend. If the cue ball comes back to the left or right of where it began, you are hitting it off-center.

## *Stop Shot Drill*

Figure 13.2 illustrates the most common of all shots—the stop shot. You must be able to execute this shot before moving on to any other drill. Set the cue ball near the center of the table as shown and drive the object ball into the corner pocket. The cue ball must stop at the point where it contacts the object ball, depicted in our diagram by the grayed-out cue ball.

Do this shot first every day until you can stop that cue ball on a dime! If you strike the cue ball somewhat below center, as shown, you will find this shot considerably easier. This allows you to hit the shot fairly gently since the slight draw will prevent the cue ball from gaining "natural roll" from the friction of contact with the cloth. The cue ball must still be sliding and not rolling when it hits the object ball or it will continue forward and follow the object ball down the table.

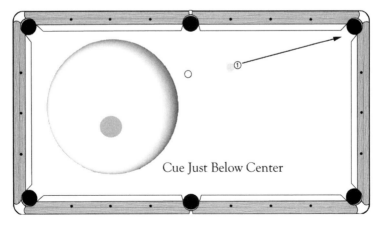

**Figure 13.2** *Stop Shot Drill.*

## Draw Shot Drill

The next shot, shown in Figure 13.3, is a definite step up in difficulty, but one you must master to progress in the game of pocket billiards. In the previous drill, the stop shot, your goal was to have the cue ball sliding when it contacted the object ball. In the draw shot, the cue ball must be spinning backward when it contacts the object ball.

Many good players can draw the cue ball, but they often do it unpredictably. That's why you want to always start off with a specific draw distance goal in mind. In this draw drill you are attempting to pocket the object ball and then draw the cue ball back to where it was when you stroked the shot.

Once you have become comfortable with this shot, you should begin to vary the distance you draw the cue ball. To become advanced in this game, you must be able to consistently draw the ball the distance of one diamond, two diamonds, three diamonds, and so on, until you can bring the ball backward whatever distance is required for the shot at hand.

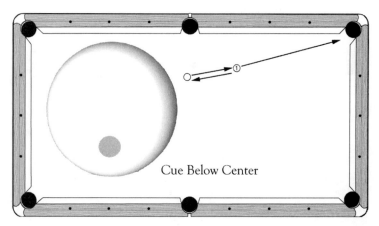

**Figure 13.3** Draw Shot Drill.

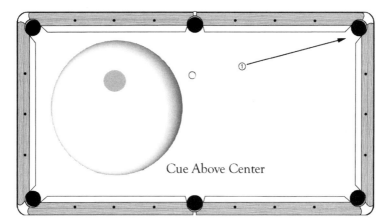

**Figure 13.4** *Follow Shot Drill.*

## Follow Shot Drill

Now that you have mastered the draw shot, the follow shot will be easy. Since it is the easiest to control, this is the shot most often used by professionals to gain position for the next ball. Practice the follow shot shown in Figure 13.4 until you can stop the cue ball at any diamond on the table. This includes having it follow to the end rail and come back up table first one, then two, then three diamonds, and so on.

## Objective for the Draw and Follow Shot Drills

Figure 13.5 shows the situation that you must be able to handle with both draw and follow. Using either top or bottom, you should be able to pocket the 1-ball and get shape on the 2-ball. Practice until you can and you will bring a confident arm to the table.

Figure 13.6 is another drill for the draw shot that will improve your skills dramatically. Make each ball in the corner pocket and draw back for shape on the next ball in the same corner. Note that if you make a mistake and get out of line for the

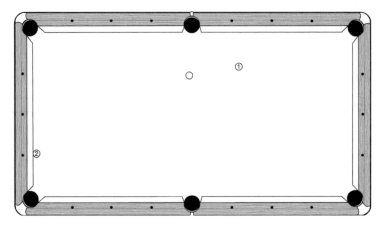

**Figure 13.5** *Draw and Follow Shot Drill.*

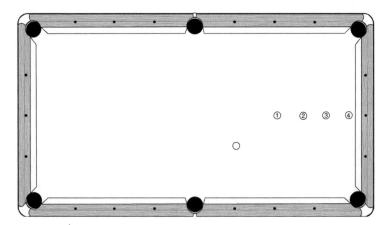

**Figure 13.6** *Additional Draw Shot Drill.*

next shot, you should pick the cue ball up and put it where you wanted it to be. This will show your subconscious the amount of correction needed for next time.

## *Speed Control Drill*

Once you understand the effect that stop, draw, and follow have on position play, it becomes important that you remember your

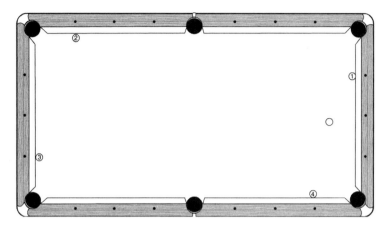

**Figure 13.7** *Speed Control Drill.*

greatest ally is still plain old speed control. No amount of English will assist you if you overstrike the shot or come up short.

Practice the drill in Figure 13.7 with no English, using only proper speed to get shape on the next shot, until your arm reliably delivers the result that you envision.

## Striking Accuracy Drill, Part I

If you find that you are lacking consistency in any of the drills thus far, your bridge hand may be either too loose or too far away from the cue ball to deliver an accurate stroke.

Set up the shot shown in Figure 13.8 and mark the position of the cue ball and object ball so that you can get them back to exactly the same spots over and over. Then mark the tangent line where the cue ball is going to come off of the object ball (a line that is exactly 90 degrees from the line of travel of the object ball). It is marked as line "T" (for *tangent*) in the diagram.

Now, and this is very important, make sure you aim the shot precisely and that the object ball goes straight into the heart of the pocket on each shot. This is no time for slop. In fact, for

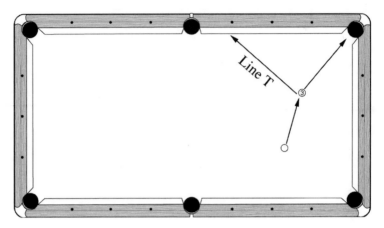

**Figure 13.8** *Striking Accuracy Drill, Part I.*

this exercise, you might want to tighten the pocket up to just over a single ball width by putting two pieces of chalk in front.

We know that if you hit that cue ball in the center and make the object ball go into the center of the pocket, the cue ball will have to travel along the tangent line (T) every time. There are no exceptions to this rule unless you don't correctly hit the cue ball, striking it either too high or too low. If your bridge length is too long for you to hit the cue ball accurately, you will vary from the tangent line and need to move the bridge hand closer to gain accuracy. If the cue ball keeps traveling to the high side (toward the pocket), then your cue stick is wandering off-center and up. If the cue ball travels to the low side of the tangent line (away from the pocket), then the cue stick is dipping before impact and you are hitting the cue ball with bottom spin.

Keep moving the bridge hand in until your object ball travels along the tangent line. You have to be able to do this to play accurate position. If you can't, the cue ball will get loose and give you many unpleasant surprises.

Don't be surprised if your proper bridge length is down around 4 inches or so. But if your bridge length gets real close and you are still not consistently moving along the tangent line, then your bridge is too loose and you need to tighten up that loop finger.

## Striking Accuracy Drill, Part II

This drill helps to continue to fine-tune that bridge length so that you will have a position game that is so predictable that it will scare you.

You are going to set up the same shot that you did for the first striking accuracy drill, again drawing line "T" to represent the tangent line. Start out with center ball hits to make sure you are at the proper bridge length. If you travel to one side or the other of the tangent line, your stroke is not accurate and you must move that bridge hand closer.

Now draw another line because you are going to add the element of English. When you must strike the cue ball off-center, your bridge changes just a bit. It tends to loosen and that can be a very deadly flaw. So in this shot, you want to hit the ball with a single tip's worth of left English. The diagram in Figure 13.9 shows where the cue ball goes with a tip of left on this shot on Ewa's table with her stroke.

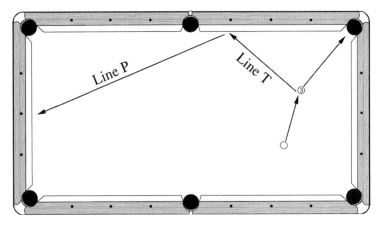

**Figure 13.9** *Striking Accuracy Drill, Part II.*

Make the shot with a tip of left and mark the path the cue ball travels off of the first rail. We have drawn this on our diagram as line "P" (for *path*). If your bridge length is proper and your bridge loop is snug and secure, the cue ball should first travel along the same line "T" as in the previous drill, strike the rail, and then travel along line "P" every time. Your line "P" will differ from the one drawn according to table conditions and stroke, but it should be consistent.

## Circle Drill

The circle drill is one of the oldest practice routines and one of the best to gain precision in cue ball control. There are many variations, but begin by placing the cue ball in the center of the circle (as shown in Figure 13.10) and attempt to bring the cue ball back inside the circle for each succeeding shot.

Don't let this one frustrate you. Even the pros have some difficulty getting all the way through the circle. The idea is to practice this drill and get farther around the circle in time.

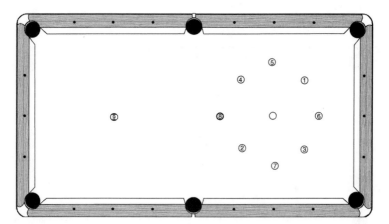

*Figure 13.10 Circle Drill.*

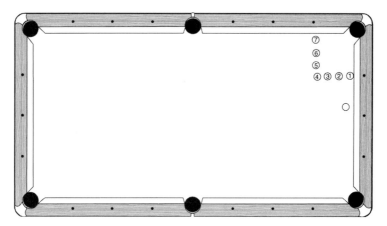

**Figure 13.11** *"L" Drill.*

## *"L" Drill*

This drill is another old favorite of the pros. Begin with the cue ball just off the rail, as shown in Figure 13.11, and then shoot each ball into the corner pocket. Draw back on each shot in order to get position that will enable you both to make the next ball and get shape for the following shot as well.

Again, this is a tough drill, but over time you should be able to see improvement in your performance. The pros can do this one pretty consistently, and they know that being able to control the cue ball over short distances is absolutely crucial to success in the game.

## *Another Speed Control Drill*

Both of the two previous drills improve your short-distance cue ball control. Now stretch out a bit and work on moving the cue ball up and down the table for shape. Place the cue ball anywhere on the table you wish to begin, as shown in Figure 13.12, and then make each ball in numerical order.

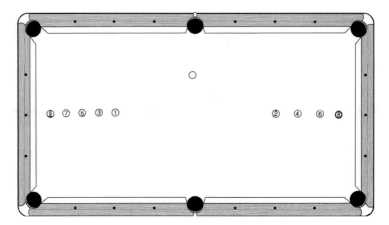

**Figure 13.12** *Another Speed Control Drill.*

Remember to visualize the exact path you want both the cue ball and the object balls to travel. Your arm will react much more reliably if you draw it a mental picture to follow.

## Position Off of the Rails Drill

Now the shots become a little tougher. You will have to be able to shoot these shots off of the rails all the time, and you need to be very comfortable with them. Most people visualize striking the rail and the ball at the same time, though the truth of the matter is that you strike the rail just a fraction before the ball.

As diagrammed in Figure 13.13, make each ball in order and get shape on the next ball. Practice this until the rail shot is as easy as a ball in the middle of the table. Actually, this shot is easier because you have an easier aiming point for reference.

## Spot Shot Drill

The spot shot doesn't come up as often in pool anymore due to rule changes that allow ball-in-hand shots. But it is still one of

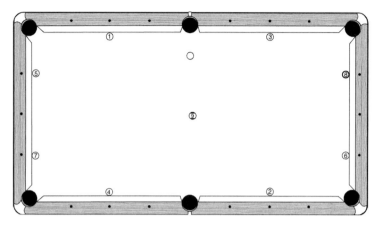

**Figure 13.13** *Position Off of the Rails Drill.*

the greatest tests of shot-making skill and a real confidence-builder. Many pros can make this shot, shown in Figure 13.14, at least 90 percent of the time.

You need to work on this shot until it is reliable. Do not forget to visualize a path for the cue ball to take after making the

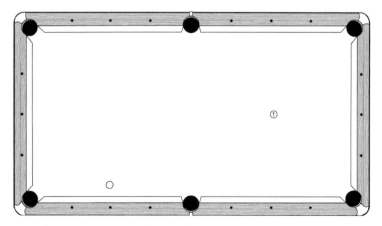

**Figure 13.14** *Spot Shot Drill.*

shot. Imagine another ball somewhere on the table for which you must play position.

## Safety Drill

Players who properly think their way through the rack know that there is a time to shoot and a time to duck. Figure 13.15 shows the perfect time to duck. There is no reasonable shot available and the safety puts your opponent at a considerable disadvantage.

It is all about playing the percentages. If the situation is such that the safety is as tough as the shot, go for the shot. It is better to go down shooting than ducking. But if the safety is obviously the wiser choice, take it every time.

## Cheating the Pocket Drill

Always remember that the pockets on a pool table are more than twice the width of a ball. This means that you do not always have to send the object ball into the center of the pocket. Often you will need to help create a little more angle for your position play by "cheating" the pocket.

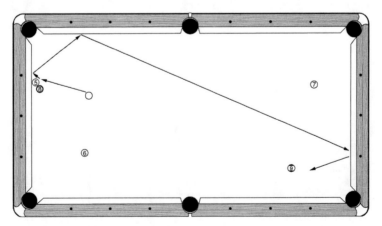

**Figure 13.15** Safety Drill.

Execute a variety of shots by striking the object ball at the various points shown in Figure 13.16. You will find that a combination of these striking points along with speed control and English will enable you to move the cue ball from here to almost any point on the table.

## *9-Ball Break Shot Drill, Part I*

The break shot is much more than just hitting the balls hard and hoping something finds a hole. It is one of the most important shots of the game, and you must plan it well. Your goal on the break shot is twofold. You must attempt to leave the cue ball somewhere near the center of the table, and you must make a ball. (See Figure 13.17.)

The reason that you must leave the cue ball near the center of the table is that this gives you the greatest possibility of having a shot on the first ball. If you lose the cue ball and it winds up behind the rack or squatting on a rail, you are hurting your chances of a run-out. Pull back on the speed of your break shot until you get to the point of control. Never hit the break shot with more force than you can control, and constantly strive to improve your control over firmer and firmer breaks.

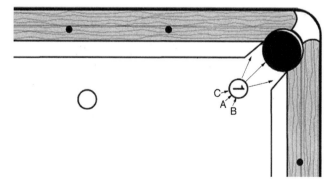

**Figure 13.16** *Cheating the Pocket Drill.*

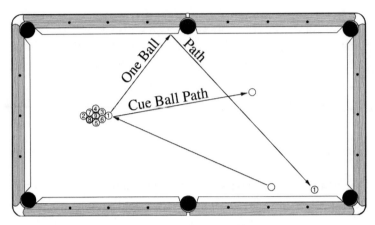

**Figure 13.17** *9-Ball Break Shot Drill, Part I.*

## 9-Ball Break Shot Drill, Part II

Once you can control the cue ball on the break, it is time to concentrate on making a ball. Figure 13.18 shows the balls you can reasonably expect to make on the break shot as well as where they will fall.

The key to making the 1-ball in the side pocket is speed control and a tight rack. Start off striking the rack very gently

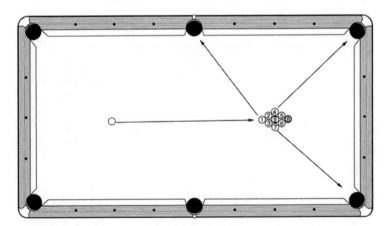

**Figure 13.18** *9-Ball Break Shot Drill, Part II.*

and watch the path that the 1-ball takes. Gradually increase your speed until the 1-ball drops in the side.

The wing balls go into the corners on the harder break shots. Give yourself a truly tight rack with no gaps and one of the wing balls should fly into the corner most times.

On break shots, pros will begin breaking with the cue ball as far as possible to one side of the table or the other and then move the cue ball along the head string until they find the point on the table that gives them the best results.

## *Planning the Table Drill*

Pool is a game for thinkers, not bangers. Take a look at Figure 13.19 and plan your run. This is what you should get into the habit of doing *before* you bend to the table after the break shot.

Make it part of your routine to plan every shot before you begin the run. Walk around the table as you do this since some shots are more easily discerned from different angles. At first your game plan will change frequently as your position play may not be perfect. Soon, however, your plans will firm up along with your game.

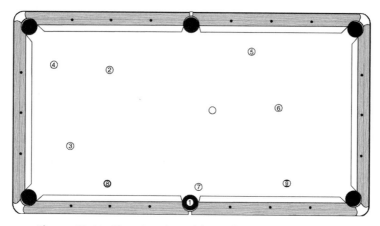

**Figure 13.19** *Planning the Table Drill.*

# Appendix
## Rules of the Game

Before venturing out to play against others, it is important that you have a good working knowledge of the rules. The rules keep everyone playing the same game and prevent misunderstandings.

Here are the General Rules of Pocket Billiards, along with the rule sets for 9-Ball and 8-Ball, as written by the World Pool-Billiard Association. These and the rules for many other games can be found in the *Billiard Congress of America Official Rules Book*. They also may be found at the association's website, WPA-Pool.com, under the tab "World Rules."

### *General Rules for Pocket Billiards*

Except when clearly contradicted by these additional rules, the General Rules of Pocket Billiards apply. These general rules apply to all pocket billiard games, UNLESS specifically noted to the contrary in the individual game rules.

## Tables, Balls, Equipment

All games described in these rules are designed for tables, balls, and equipment meeting the standards prescribed in the WPA Equipment Specifications.

## Racking the Balls

When racking the balls a triangle must be used, and the apex ball is to be spotted on the foot spot. All the balls must be lined up behind the apex ball and pressed together so that they all have contact with each other.

## Striking Cue Ball

Legal shots require that the cue ball be struck only with the cue tip. Failure to meet this requirement is a foul.

## Calling Shots

For games of call-shot a player may shoot any ball he chooses, but before he shoots, must designate the called ball and called pocket. He need not indicate any detail such as kisses, caroms, combinations, or cushions (all of which are legal). Any additionally pocketed ball(s) on a legal stroke is counted in the shooter's favor.

## Failure to Pocket a Ball

If a player fails to pocket a ball on a legal shot, then the player's inning is over, and it is the opponent's turn at the table.

## Lag for Break

The following procedure is used for the lag for the opening break. Each player should use balls of equal size and weight (preferably cue balls but, when not available, nonstriped object balls). With the balls in hand behind the head string, one player to the left and one to the right of the head spot, the balls are shot simultaneously to the foot cushion and back to the head end of the table. The player whose ball is the closest to the innermost edge of the head cushion wins the lag. The lagged ball must contact the foot cushion at least once. Other cushion contacts are immaterial, except as prohibited below. It is an automatic loss of the lag if:

(a) The ball crosses into the opponent's half of the table,

(b) The ball fails to contact the foot cushion,

(c) The ball drops into a pocket,

(d) The ball jumps the table,

(e) The ball touches the long cushion,

(f) The ball rests within the corner pocket and past the nose of the head cushion, or

(g) The ball contacts the foot rail more than once.

If both players violate automatic-loss lag rules, or if the referee is unable to determine which ball is closer, the lag is a tie and is replayed.

## Opening Break Shot

The opening break shot is determined by either lag or lot. (The lag for break procedure is required for formal competition.) The player winning the lag or lot has the choice of performing the opening break shot or assigning it to the opponent.

## Cue Ball on Opening Break

The opening break shot is taken with cue ball in hand behind the head string. The object balls are positioned according to specific game rules. On the opening break, the game is considered to have commenced once the cue ball has been struck by the cue tip.

## Deflecting the Cue Ball on the Game's Opening Break

On the break shot, stopping or deflecting the cue ball after it has crossed the head string and prior to hitting the racked balls is considered a foul and loss of turn. The opponent has the option of receiving cue ball in hand behind the head string or passing the cue ball in hand behind the head string back to the offending player. (Exception: 9-Ball, see "Cue Ball in Hand Anywhere on the Table.") A warning must be given that a second violation during the match will result in the loss of the match by forfeiture.

## Cue Ball in Hand Behind the Head String

This situation applies in specific games whereby the opening break is administered or a player's scratching is penalized by the incoming player having cue ball in hand behind the head string. The incoming player may place the cue ball anywhere behind the head string. The shooting player may shoot at any object ball as long as the base of the object ball is on or below the head string. He may not shoot at any ball, the base of which is above the head string, unless he first shoots the cue ball below the head string and then by hitting a rail causes the cue ball to come back above the head string and hit the object ball. The base of the ball (the point of the ball touching the table) determines whether it is above or below the head string. If the incoming player inadvertently places the cue ball on or below the head string, the referee or the opposing player must inform the shooting player of improper positioning of the cue ball before the shot is made. If the opposing player does not so inform the shooting player before the shot is made, the shot is considered legal. If the shooting player is informed of improper positioning, he must then reposition the cue ball. If a player positions the cue ball completely and obviously outside the kitchen and shoots the cue ball, it is a foul. When the cue ball is in hand behind the head string, it remains in hand (not in play) until the player drives the cue ball past the head string by striking it with his cue tip. The cue ball may be adjusted by the player's hand, cue, etc., so long as it remains in hand. Once the cue ball is in play per the above, it may not be impeded in any way by the player; to do so is to commit a foul. Additionally, if the shot fails to contact a legal object ball or fails to drive the cue ball over the head string, the shot is a foul and the opposing player has ball in hand according to the specific game rules.

## Pocketed Balls

A ball is considered pocketed if as a result of an otherwise legal shot, it drops off the bed of the table into the pocket and remains there. (A ball that drops out of a ball return system onto the floor is not to be construed as a ball that has not remained pocketed.) A ball that rebounds from a pocket back onto the table bed is not a pocketed ball.

## Position of Balls

The position of a ball is judged by where its base (or center) rests.

## Foot on Floor

A player must have at least one foot in contact with the floor at the moment the cue tip contacts the cue ball, or the shot is a foul. Foot attire must be normal in regard to size, shape, and manner in which it is worn.

## Shooting with Balls in Motion

It is a foul if a player shoots while the cue ball or any object ball is in motion (a spinning ball is in motion).

## Completion of Stroke

A stroke is not complete (and therefore is not counted) until all balls on the table have become motionless after the stroke (a spinning ball is in motion).

## Head String Defined

The area behind the head string does not include the head string. Thus, an object ball that is dead center on the head string is playable when specific game rules require that a player must shoot at a ball past the head string. Likewise, the cue ball when being put in play behind the head string (cue ball in hand behind the head string), may not be placed directly on the head string; it must be behind it.

## General Rules, All Fouls

Though the penalties for fouls differ from game to game, the following apply to all fouls:

(a) Player's inning ends,

(b) If on a stroke, the stroke is invalid and any pocketed balls are not counted to the shooter's credit, and

(c) Any ball(s) is respotted only if the rules of the specific game require it.

### Failure to Contact Object Ball

It is a foul if on a stroke the cue ball fails to make contact with any legal object ball first. Playing away from a touching ball does not constitute having hit that ball.

### Legal Shot

Unless otherwise stated in a specific game rule, a player must cause the cue ball to contact a legal object ball and then:

(a) Pocket a numbered ball or

(b) Cause the cue ball or any numbered ball to contact a cushion or any part of the rail. Failure to meet these requirements is a foul.

### Cue Ball Scratch

It is a foul (scratch) if on a stroke, the cue ball is pocketed. If the cue ball touches an object ball that was already pocketed (for example, in a pocket full of object balls), the shot is a foul.

## Fouls by Touching Balls

It is a foul to strike, touch, or in any way make contact with the cue ball in play or any object balls in play with anything (the body, clothing, chalk, mechanical bridge, cue shaft, etc.) except the cue tip (while attached to the cue shaft), which may contact the cue ball in the execution of a legal shot. Whenever a referee is presiding over a match, any object ball moved during a standard foul must be returned as closely as possible to its original position as judged by the referee, and the incoming player does not have the option of restoration.

## Foul by Placement

Touching any object ball with the cue ball while it is in hand is a foul.

## Fouls by Double Hits

If the cue ball is touching the required object ball prior to the shot, the player may shoot toward it, providing that any normal stroke is employed. If the cue stick strikes the cue ball more than once on a shot, or if the cue stick is in contact with the cue ball when or after the cue ball contacts an object ball, the shot is foul. If a third ball is close by, care should be taken not to foul that ball under the first part of this rule.

## Push Shot Fouls

It is a foul if the cue ball is pushed by the cue tip, with contact being maintained for more than the momentary time commensurate with a stroked shot. (Such shots are usually referred to as push shots.)

## Player Responsibility Fouls

The player is responsible for chalk, bridges, files, and any other items or equipment he brings to, uses at, or causes to approximate the table. If he drops a piece of chalk or knocks off a mechanical bridge head, as examples, he is guilty of a foul should such an object make contact with any ball in play (or the cue ball only if no referee is presiding over the match).

## Illegal Jumping of Ball

It is a foul if a player strikes the cue ball below center ("digs under" it) and intentionally causes it to rise off the bed of the table in an effort to clear an obstructing ball. Such jumping action may occasionally occur accidentally, and such "jumps" are not to be considered fouls on their face; they may still be ruled foul strokes, if for example, the ferrule or cue shaft makes contact with the cue ball in the course of the shot.

## Jump Shots

Unless otherwise stated in rules for a specific game it is legal to cause the cue ball to rise off the bed of the table by elevating the cue stick on the shot, and forcing the cue ball to rebound from the bed of the table. Any miscue when executing a jump shot is a foul.

## Balls Jumped off Table

Balls coming to rest other than on the bed of the table after a stroke (on the cushion top, rail surface, floor, etc.) are considered jumped balls. Balls may bounce on the cushion tops and rails of the table in play without being jumped balls if they return to the bed of the table under their own power and without touching anything not a part of the table. The table shall consist of the permanent part of the table proper. (Balls that strike or touch anything not a part of the table, such as the light fixture, chalk on the rails and cushion tops, etc., shall be considered jumped balls even though they might return to the bed of the table after contacting items which are not parts of the table proper.) In all pocket billiard games, when a stroke results in the cue ball or any object ball being a jumped ball off the table, the stroke is a foul. All jumped object balls are spotted (except in 9-Ball and in 8-Ball) when all balls have stopped moving. See specific game rules for putting the cue ball in play after a jumped cue ball foul.

## Special Intentional Foul Penalty

The cue ball in play shall not be intentionally struck with anything other than a cue's attached tip (such as the ferrule, shaft, etc.). While such contact is automatically a foul under the provisions of these rules, if the referee deems the contact to be intentional, he shall warn the player once during a match that a second violation during that match will result in the loss of the match by forfeiture. If a second violation does occur, the match must be forfeited.

## One Foul Limit

Unless specific game rules dictate otherwise, only one foul is assessed on a player in each inning; if different penalties can apply, the most severe penalty is the factor determining which foul is assessed.

## Balls Moving Spontaneously

If a ball shifts, settles, turns, or otherwise moves "by itself," the ball shall remain in the position it assumed and play continues. A hanging ball that falls into a pocket "by itself" after being motionless for 5 seconds or longer shall be replaced as closely as possible to its position prior to falling, and play shall continue. If an object ball drops into a pocket "by itself" as a player shoots at it, so that the cue ball passes over the spot the ball had been on, unable to hit it, the cue ball and object ball are to be replaced to their positions prior to the stroke, and the player may shoot again. Any other object balls disturbed on the stroke are also to be replaced to their original positions before the shooter replays.

## Spotting Balls

When specific game rules call for spotting balls, they shall be replaced on the table on the long string after the stroke is complete. A single ball is placed on the foot spot; if more than one ball is to be spotted, they are placed on the long string in ascending numerical order, beginning on the foot spot and advancing toward the foot rail. When balls on or near the foot spot or long string interfere with the spotting of balls, the balls to be spotted are placed on the long string as close as possible to the foot spot without moving the interfering balls. Spotted balls are to be placed as close as possible or frozen (at the referee's discretion) to such interfering balls, except when the cue ball is interfering; balls to be spotted against the cue ball are placed as close as possible without being frozen. If there is insufficient room on the long string between the foot spot and the foot rail cushion for balls that must be spotted, such balls are then placed on the extension of the long string "in front" of the foot spot (between the foot spot and the center spot), as near as possible to the foot spot and in the same numerical order as if they were spotted "behind" the foot spot (lowest numbered ball closest to the foot spot).

### Jawed Balls

If two or more balls are locked between the jaws or sides of the pocket, with one or more suspended in air, the referee shall inspect the balls in position and follow this procedure: he shall visually (or physically if he desires) project each ball directly downward from its locked position; any ball that in his judgment would fall in the pocket if so moved directly downward is a pocketed ball, while any ball that would come to rest on the bed of the table is not pocketed. The balls are then placed according to the referee's assessment, and play continues according to specific game rules as if no locking or jawing of balls had occurred.

### Additional Pocketed Balls

If extra balls are pocketed on a legal scoring stroke, they are counted in accord with the scoring rules for the particular game.

### Nonplayer Interference

If the balls are moved (or a player bumped such that play is directly affected) by a nonplayer during the match, the balls shall be replaced as near as possible to their original positions immediately prior to the incident, and play shall resume with no penalty on the player affected. If the match is officiated, the referee shall replace the balls. This rule shall also apply to "act of God" interference, such as earthquake, hurricane, light fixture falling, power failure, etc. If the balls cannot be restored to their original positions, replay the game with the original player breaking. This rule is not applicable to 14.1 Continuous where the game consists of successive racks; the rack in progress will be discontinued and a completely new rack will be started with the requirements of the normal opening break (players lag for break). Scoring of points is to be resumed at the score as it stood at the moment of game disruption.

### Breaking Subsequent Racks

In a match that consists of short rack games, the winner of each game breaks in the next. The following are common options that may be designated by tournament officials in advance:

(a)  Players alternate break.

(b)  Loser breaks.

(c)  Player trailing in game count breaks the next game.

### Play by Innings

During the course of play, players alternate turns (innings) at the table, with a player's inning ending when he either fails to legally pocket a ball or fouls. When an inning ends free of a foul, the incoming player accepts the table in position.

### Object Ball Frozen to Cushion or Cue Ball

This rule applies to any shot where the cue ball's first contact with a ball is with one that is frozen to a cushion or to the cue ball itself. After the cue ball makes contact with the frozen object ball, the shot must result in either:

(a) A ball being pocketed, or

(b) The cue ball contacting a cushion, or

(c) The frozen ball being caused to contact a cushion attached to a separate rail, or

(d) Another object ball being caused to contact a cushion with which it was not already in contact.

Failure to satisfy one of those four requirements is a foul. (Note: 14.1 Continuous and other games specify additional requirements and applications of this rule; see specific game rules.) A ball which is touching a cushion at the start of a shot and then is forced into a cushion attached to the same rail is not considered to have been driven to that cushion unless it leaves the cushion, contacts another ball, and then contacts the cushion again. An object ball is not considered frozen to a cushion unless it is examined and announced as such by either the referee or one of the players prior to that object ball being involved in a shot.

## Playing from Behind the String

When a player has the cue ball in hand behind the head string (in the kitchen), he must drive the cue ball to a point across the head string before it contacts either a cushion, an object ball, or returns to the kitchen. Failure to do so is a foul if a referee is presiding over a match. If no referee, the opponent has the option to either call it a foul or to require the offending player to replay the shot again with the balls restored to their positions prior to the shot (and with no foul penalty imposed). Exception: if an object ball lies on or outside the head string (and is thus playable) but so close that the cue ball contacts it before the cue ball is out of the kitchen, the ball can be legally played, and will be considered to have crossed the head string. If, with cue ball in hand behind the head string and while the shooter is attempting a legitimate shot, the cue ball accidentally hits a ball behind the head string, and the cue ball crosses the line, it is a foul. If with cue ball in hand behind the head string, the shooter causes the cue ball to hit an object ball accidentally, and the cue ball does not cross the head string, the following applies: the incoming player has the option of calling a foul and having cue ball in hand, or having the balls returned to their original position, and having the offending player replay the shot. If a player under the same conditions intentionally causes the cue ball to contact an object ball behind the head string, it is unsportsmanlike conduct.

### Cue Ball in Hand Foul

During cue ball in hand placement, the player may use his hand or any part of his cue (including the tip) to position the cue ball. When placing the cue ball in position, any forward stroke motion of the cue stick contacting the cue ball will be considered a foul if not a legal shot.

### Interference

If the nonshooting player distracts his opponent or interferes with his play, he has fouled. If a player shoots out of turn, or moves any ball except during his inning, it is considered to be interference.

### Devices

Players are not allowed to use a ball, the triangle, or any other width-measuring device to see if the cue ball or an object ball would travel through a gap, etc. Only the cue stick may be used as an aid to judge gaps or as an aid to aligning a shot, so long as the cue is held by the hand. To do so otherwise is a foul and unsportsmanlike conduct.

### Illegal Marking

If a player intentionally marks the table in any way to assist in executing the shot, including the placement of chalk, it is a foul.

## *8-Ball*

Except when clearly contradicted by these additional rules, the General Rules of Pocket Billiards apply.

### Object of the Game

8-Ball is a call shot game played with a cue ball and 15 object balls, numbered 1 through 15. One player must pocket balls of the group numbered 1 through 7 (solid colors), while the other player has 9 through 15 (stripes). The player pocketing either group first and then legally pocketing the 8-ball wins the game.

### Call Shot

In Call Shot, obvious balls and pockets do not have to be indicated. It is the opponent's right to ask which ball and pocket if he is unsure of the shot. Bank shots and combination shots are not considered obvious, and care should be taken in calling both the object ball and the intended pocket. When calling the shot, it is never necessary to indicate details such as the number of cushions, banks, kisses, caroms, etc. Any balls pocketed on a foul remain pocketed, regardless of whether they belong to the shooter or the opponent. The opening break is not a "called shot." Any player performing a break shot in 8-Ball may continue to shoot so long as any object ball is legally pocketed on the break.

### Racking the Balls

The balls are racked in a triangle at the foot of the table with the 8-ball in the center of the triangle, the first ball of the rack on the foot spot, a stripe ball in one corner of the rack and a solid ball in the other corner.

### Order of the Break

Winner of the lag has the option to break. In 8-Ball the winner of each game breaks in the next unless otherwise specified by the tournament organizer. The following are common options that may be designated by tournament officials in advance:

(a) Players alternate break.

(b) Loser breaks.

(c) Player trailing in game count breaks the next game.

## Legal Break Shot

(Defined) To execute a legal break, the breaker (with the cue ball behind the head string) must either (1) pocket a ball or (2) drive at least four numbered balls to the rail. When the breaker fails to make a legal break, it is a foul and the incoming player has the option of (1) accepting the table in position and shooting or (2) having the balls reracked and having the option of shooting the opening break or allowing the offending player to rebreak.

## Scratch on a Legal Break

If a player scratches on a legal break shot, (1) all balls pocketed remain pocketed (exception, the 8-ball), (2) it is a foul, (3) the table is open. Please note: The incoming player has cue ball in hand behind the head string and may not shoot an object ball that is behind the head string, unless he first shoots the cue ball past the head string and causes the cue ball to come back behind the head string and hit the object ball.

## Object Balls Jumped off Table on the Break

If a player jumps an object ball off the table on the break shot, it is a foul and the incoming player has the option of (1) accepting the table in position and shooting, or (2) taking cue ball in hand behind the head string and shooting.

## 8-Ball Pocketed on the Break

If the 8-ball is pocketed on the break, breaker may ask for a rerack or have the 8-ball spotted and continue shooting. If the breaker scratches while pocketing the 8-ball on the break, the incoming player has the option of a rerack or having the 8-ball spotted and begin shooting with ball in hand behind the head string.

## Open Table

(Defined) The table is "open" when the choice of groups (stripes or solids) has not yet been determined. When the table is open, it is legal to hit a solid first to make a stripe or vice versa. Note: The table is always open immediately after the break shot. When the table is open, it is legal to hit any solid or stripe first in the process of pocketing the called stripe or solid. However, when the table is open and the 8-ball is the first ball contacted, it is a foul and no stripe or solid may be scored in favor of the shooter. The shooter loses his turn; the incoming player is awarded cue ball in hand; any balls pocketed remain pocketed; and the incoming player addresses the balls with the table still open. On an open table, all illegally pocketed balls remain pocketed.

## Choice of Group

The choice of stripes or solids is not determined on the break even if balls are made from only one or both groups, because the table is always open immediately after the break shot. The choice of group is determined only when a player legally pockets a called object ball after the break shot.

## Legal Shot

(Defined) On all shots (except on the break and when the table is open), the shooter must hit one of his group of balls first and (1) pocket a numbered ball or (2) cause the cue ball or any numbered ball to contact a rail. Please note: It is permissible for the shooter to bank the cue ball off a rail before contacting the object ball; however, after contact with the object ball, an object ball must be pocketed, or the cue ball or any numbered ball must contact a rail. Failure to meet these requirements is a foul.

## "Safety" Shot

For tactical reasons, a player may choose to pocket an obvious object ball and also discontinue a turn at the table by declaring "safety" in advance. A safety shot is defined as a legal shot. If the shooting player intends to play safe by pocketing an obvious object ball, then prior to the shot, the shooter must declare a "safety" to the opponent. It is the shooter's responsibility to make the opponent aware of the intended safety shot. If this is not done, and one of the shooter's object balls is pocketed, the shooter will be required to shoot again. Any ball pocketed on a safety shot remains pocketed.

## Scoring

A player is entitled to continue shooting until failing to legally pocket a ball of his group. After a player has legally pocketed all of his group of balls, he shoots to pocket the 8-ball.

## Foul Penalty

Opposing player gets cue ball in hand. This means that the player can place the cue ball anywhere on the table (does not have to be behind the head string except on opening break). This rule prevents a player from making intentional fouls which would put an opponent at a disadvantage. With "cue ball in hand," the player may use a hand or any part of a cue (including the tip) to position the cue ball. When placing the cue ball in position, any forward stroke motion contacting the cue ball will be a foul, if not a legal shot.

## Combination Shots

Combination shots are allowed; however, the 8-ball can't be used as a first ball in the combination. Should such contact occur on the 8-ball, it is a foul.

## Illegally Pocketed Balls

An object ball is considered to be illegally pocketed when (1) that object ball is pocketed on the same shot a foul is committed, or (2) the called ball did not go in the designated pocket, or (3) a safety is called prior to the shot. Illegally pocketed balls remain pocketed and are scored in favor of the shooter controlling that specific group of balls, solids or stripes.

## Object Balls Jumped off the Table

If any object ball is jumped off the table, it is a foul and loss of turn, unless it is the 8-ball, which is a loss of game. Any jumped object balls are not respotted.

## Jump and Masse Shot Foul

While "cue ball fouls only" is the rule of play when a match is not presided over by a referee, a player should be aware that it will be considered a cue ball foul if during an attempt to jump, curve, or masse the cue ball over or around an impeding numbered ball that is not a legal object ball, the impeding ball moves (regardless of whether it was moved by a hand, cue stick follow-through, or bridge).

## Playing the 8-Ball

When the 8-ball is the legal object ball, a scratch or foul is not loss of game if the 8-ball is not pocketed or jumped from the table. Incoming player has cue ball in hand. Note: A combination shot can never be used to legally pocket the 8-ball, except when the 8-ball is the first ball contacted in the shot sequence.

## Loss of Game

A player loses the game by committing any of the following infractions:

1. Fouls when pocketing the 8-ball (exception: see 8-Ball Pocketed on the Break).

2. Pockets the 8-ball on the same stroke as the last of his group of balls.

3. Jumps the 8-ball off the table at any time.

4. Pockets the 8-ball in a pocket other than the one designated.

5. Pockets the 8-ball when it is not the legal object ball.

Note: All infractions must be called before another shot is taken, or else it will be deemed that no infraction occurred.

## Stalemated Game

If, after three consecutive turns at the table by each player (six turns total), the referee judges (or if no referee, both players agree) that attempting to pocket or move an object ball will result in loss of game, the balls will be reracked with the original breaker of the stalemated game breaking again. The stalemate rule may be applied regardless of the number of balls on the table. Please note: Three consecutive fouls by one player in 8-Ball is not a loss of game.

# 9-Ball

Except when clearly contradicted by these additional rules, the General Rules of Pocket Billiards apply.

## Object of the Game

9-Ball is played with nine object balls numbered one through nine and a cue ball. On each shot, the first ball the cue ball contacts must be the lowest numbered ball on the table, but the balls need not be pocketed in order. If a player pockets any ball on a legal shot, he remains at the table for another shot and continues until missing, committing a foul, or winning the game by pocketing the 9-ball. After a miss, the incoming player must shoot from the position left by the previous player, but after any foul the incoming player may start with the cue ball anywhere on the table. Players are not required to call any shot. A match ends when one of the players has won the required number of games.

## Racking the Balls

The object balls are racked in a diamond shape, with the 1-ball at the top of the diamond and on the foot spot, the 9-ball in the center of the diamond, and the other balls in random order, racked as tightly as possible. The game begins with cue ball in hand behind the head string.

## Order of the Break

Winner of the lag has the option to break. In 9-Ball the winner of each game breaks in the next unless otherwise specified by the tournament organizer. The following are common options that may be designated by tournament officials in advance:

(a) Players alternate break.

(b) Loser breaks.

(c) Player trailing in game count breaks the next game.

## Legal Break Shot

The rules governing the break shot are the same as for other shots except:

1. The breaker must strike the 1-ball first and either pocket a ball or drive at least four numbered balls to the rail.

2. If the cue ball is pocketed or driven off the table, or the requirements of the opening break are not met, it is a foul and the incoming player has cue ball in hand anywhere on the table.

3. If on the break shot, the breaker causes an object ball to jump off the table, it is a foul and the incoming player has cue ball in hand anywhere on the table. The object ball is not respotted (exception: if the object ball is the 9-ball, it is respotted).

## Continuing Play

On the shot immediately following a legal break, the shooter may play a "push out." If the breaker pockets one or more balls on a legal break, he continues to shoot until he misses, fouls, or wins the game. If the player misses or fouls, the other player begins an inning and shoots until missing, committing a foul, or winning. The game ends when the 9-ball is pocketed on a legal shot, or the game is forfeited for a serious infraction of the rules.

## Push Out

The player who shoots the shot immediately after a legal break may play a push out in an attempt to move the cue ball into a better position for the option that follows. On a push out, the cue ball is not required to contact any object ball nor any rail, but all other foul rules still apply. The player must announce the intention of playing a push out before the shot, or the shot is considered to be a normal shot. Any ball pocketed on a push out does not count and remains pocketed except the 9-ball. Following a legal push out, the incoming player is permitted to shoot from that position or to pass the shot back to the player who pushed out. A push out is not considered to be a foul as long as no rule is violated. An illegal push out is penalized according to the type of foul committed. After a player scratches on the break shot, the incoming player cannot play a push out.

## Fouls

When a player commits a foul, he must relinquish his run at the table and no balls pocketed on the foul shot are respotted (exception: if a pocketed ball is the 9-ball, it is respotted). The incoming player is awarded ball in hand; prior to his first shot he may place the cue ball anywhere on the table. If a player commits several fouls on one shot, they are counted as only one foul.

## Bad Hit

If the first object ball contacted by the cue ball is not the lowest numbered ball on the table, the shot is foul.

## No Rail

If no object ball is pocketed, failure to drive the cue ball or any numbered ball to a rail after the cue ball contacts the object ball is a foul.

## In Hand

When the cue ball is in hand, the player may place the cue ball anywhere on the bed of the table, except in contact with an object ball. The player may continue to adjust the position of the cue ball until shooting.

## Object Balls Jumped off the Table

An unpocketed ball is considered to be driven off the table if it comes to rest other than on the bed of the table. It is a foul to drive an object ball off the table. The jumped object ball(s) is not respotted (exception: if the object ball is the 9-ball, it is respotted) and play continues.

## Jump and Masse Shot Foul

If a match is not refereed, it will be considered a cue ball foul if during an attempt to jump, curve, or masse the cue ball over or around an impeding numbered ball, the impeding ball moves (regardless of whether it was moved by a hand, cue stick follow-through, or bridge).

## Three Consecutive Fouls

If a player fouls three consecutive times on three successive shots without making an intervening legal shot, the game is lost. The three fouls must occur in one game. The warning must be given between the second and third fouls. A player's inning begins when it is legal to take a shot and ends at the end of a shot on which he misses, fouls, or wins, or when he fouls between shots.

## End of Game

On the opening break, the game is considered to have commenced once the cue ball has been struck by the cue tip. The 1-ball must be legally contacted on the break shot. The game ends at the end of a legal shot which pockets the 9-ball, or when a player forfeits the game as the result of a foul.

# Glossary

**Ball in Hand:** As penalty for most fouls, the incoming player has "ball in hand." He is allowed to place the cue ball anywhere on the playing surface prior to executing his first shot.

**BCA:** The Billiard Congress of America. The BCA is the governing body of pocket billiards in the United States as recognized by the World Pool-Billiard Association (WPA).

**Bridge:** The foundation upon which the shaft rests and slides, created by the nonshooting hand or a mechanical device of the same name.

**Butt:** The larger half of a two-piece cue. The section of the cue stick that contains the grip and any decorative inlays.

**Draw:** Striking the cue ball below the center line, which results in backspin being imparted to the cue ball. As a result, the cue ball comes back toward the shooter after contact with the object ball.

**English:** Striking the cue ball either right or left of the center line. A cue ball struck on the right will alter its path to the right after contacting a cushion. A ball struck on the left will alter its path to the left.

**Ferrule:** The hollow shaft of phenolic resin, fiber, ivory, or similar material that is placed on the end of the shaft of the cue directly behind the cue tip to absorb the shock of the hit and protect the end of the shaft.

**Follow:** The effect that topspin has on the shot. A cue ball struck above the center line will tend to continue forward after contact with the object ball.

**Frozen:** Another term for *touching*. Two balls are frozen when they are touching. A ball is frozen to the rail when it is in contact with that rail.

**Head String:** The breaking area of the table; a line drawn across the table that connects the second diamond on each side of the table.

**Kitchen:** The area of the pool table behind the head string.

**Lag Shot:** The opening shot in tournament play. Each player attempts to drive a ball to the end rail where it rebounds and comes back to the head of the table. The player landing closest to the head rail wins the lag and the honor of the first break shot.

**Muscle Memory:** A term used to refer to the training of a muscle to perform a repetitive task, such as a pool stroke, golf swing, or bat swing in baseball.

**Rail:** The raised sides of the pool table that contain the playing area. Also known as *cushions*.

**Shaft:** The smaller section on a two-piece cue.

**Snooker:** A cue sport made popular by British troops throughout the world during the period of colonialism. Played with 15 red balls and 6 numbered balls on a 6-by-12-foot table containing rounded pockets.

**Steering:** The act of taking the wrist out of the line of the shot after contact.

**Stop Shot:** A shot where the cue ball stops upon contact with the object ball.

**Taper:** The shafts of all pool cues are tapered. They begin as a smaller diameter (usually around 13 mm) at the cue tip and graduate along their length to match the diameter of the butt where the two pieces screw together. There are many different styles of taper, and they all have an effect upon the playing characteristics of the cue.

**Tip:** The leather point on the cue that makes contact with the cue ball.

**WPA:** The World Pool-Billiard Association. The international governing body of pocket billiards.

**WPBA:** Women's Professional Billiard Association. The professional organization that governs women's professional pool in the United States.

# Index

# About the Authors

**S**teve Mizerak is the youngest member ever inducted into the Billiard Congress of America Hall of Fame and has played championship pool for nearly 50 years. A former high school teacher in New Jersey, Steve won four consecutive U.S. Open 14:1 titles and has twice won the U.S. Open 9-Ball Championship. He is a three-time World Pocket Billiard Champion and holds more than 80 first-place finishes in world-class tournaments.

Steve has a high run of 421 consecutive balls in 14:1 and has appeared in two movies (*The Color of Money* and *The Baltimore Bullet*) as well as on "ABC Wide World of Sports" and "CBS Sports Spectacular." *Quick-Start Guide to Pocket Billiards* is his sixth book, and he has produced three videotapes on billiards. The founder and moving force behind the Senior Tour, Steve also has been active for many years in the billiard supply business with his signature line of products.

Steve can now be found running his new billiard room and sports bar, Steve Mizerak's Billiards, 914 Park Avenue, Lake Park, Florida.

*Steve Mizerak.*     *Ewa Mataya Laurance.*     *Jerry Forsyth.*

**Ewa Mataya Laurance** is one of the most well-known and recognizable stars in the history of pocket billiards. She is a past winner of multiple World Championships, including the sport's biggest prize, the WPA World 9-Ball Championship, and America's most prestigious prizes, the U.S. Open 9-Ball title (twice) and the WPBA National 9-Ball Championship. As one of only a handful of players to win all of the sport's major titles, Ewa is in elite company. Ewa is a two-time *Pool & Billiard Magazine* Player of the Year and is a recipient of the WPBA Sportsperson of the Year award and the Billiard Bowling Institute of America (BBIA) Industry Service Award. She currently serves as the President of the WPBA.

Ewa started playing pocket billiards in her native town of Gavle, Sweden, at age 14. In 1981, at age 17, she won the European Championship in Bern, Switzerland, and later that same year, she was asked to represent Europe at the World Championships in New York City. It was at that point that she made the decision to make the United States her home. Since then, Ewa has not only been successfully competing on the Women's Professional Tour, but has become widely recognized as the international ambassador for the sport, promoting pocket billiards worldwide.

In addition, Ewa has appeared on numerous television shows, including "Live with Regis and Kathie Lee," "Late Night with David Letterman," "The Today Show," and "Dennis Miller." Ewa also has been featured in a cover article in the prestigious *New York Times Magazine* as well as in a number of articles in such magazines as *People, Sports Illustrated,* and *Glamour* magazine. She has starred in national commercials for Brunswick Billiards and No Nonsense Pantyhose.

Currently, Ewa writes a monthly column for *Pool & Billiard Magazine. Quick-Start Guide to Pocket Billiards* is her third book. Besides playing on the WPBA Tour, Ewa spends a great deal of the year performing shows and trick shot exhibitions across the United States and around the world. Ewa is sponsored on tour by Brunswick Billiards, their only Professional Player Representative. She currently resides in Myrtle Beach, South Carolina, with her husband, Mitch, and daughter, Nikki.

**Jerry Forsyth** is the Tournament Editor of *Pool & Billiard Magazine* and travels the world attending every major billiard competition in that capacity. He is a member of the Tableshakers, a four-time Texas State Championship 9-Ball team, and he won the Texas State Doubles Championship in 1996. In addition, he competes on Steve's Senior Tour.

Jerry also does television broadcast commentary for British Sky Broadcasting at both the Mosconi Cup Championships, held annually in London, England, and the World Pool-Billiard Association World 9-Ball Championships, held in Cardiff, Wales. Additionally, he is a member of the billiards broadcast team for TSN Network of Toronto, Canada, and assists in their efforts with the Border Battle team billiards competitions and similar broadcasts.